WOO
HEATHS AND HEDGES

WOODLANDS, HEATHS AND HEDGES

A POPULAR DESCRIPTION OF

TREES, SHRUBS, WILD FRUITS, ETC

WITH NOTICES OF THEIR INSECT INHABITANTS

BY W. S. COLEMAN

MEMBER OF THE ENTOMOLOGICAL SOCIETY OF LONDON

With Illustrations Printed in Colours

Tynron Press, Scotland

First published in 1860

This edition first published in 1990 by
Tynron Press
Stenhouse
Thornhill
Dumfriesshire DG3 4LD

ISBN 1-871948-81-9

All rights reserved

Cover by Hazel McIntosh
Printed in Singapore by General Printing Services Pte Ltd

PREFACE

In that pleasant and popular little work by the Rev. J. G. Wood, entitled "Common Objects of the Country," the author has proved how lively an interest may be imparted by a familiar yet accurate account of some of the most ordinary productions of nature, such as are daily to be seen around us,—the subjects so happily treated of in its pages being selected almost exclusively from among the insect tribes and minor animals. The limited compass of a pocket volume could, however, embrace a small proportion only of the multitudinous objects which give animation to the country, while many departments of natural history, both in the animal and vegetable kingdoms, were necessarily omitted altogether.

It occurred to the publishers of the above-mentioned work, that, among the various rural topics thus left open, the subject of *"British Trees and Shrubs,"* though naturally one of prominent interest, was yet one on which there existed no illustrated work apart from the cyclopædic form; and therefore, in the belief that a

PREFACE.

popular treatise supplying this manifest *desideratum*, would prove to be generally acceptable, they applied to the writer of the present volume to undertake the execution of their projected design. His own experience confirms the very general belief that the majority of ramblers in the country, even inclusive of those furnished with some general botanical knowledge, are usually quite at a loss, when called upon to name the various wild trees and shrubs they meet with, or how to discriminate between them. Most people can, certainly, recognize the *Oak*, especially if they get a sight of its acorns. Some, too, will probably call an *Elm* by its right name, and so with three or four others of our most familiar trees; but as to the distinction between the *Beech* and the *Hornbeam*, for instance, they will probably be quite at fault, or only make a vague guess at most; while the less frequent trees are to them utterly nameless and unknown. Although the knowledge of names merely is a very poor acquisition, yet it is obvious enough that the first essential step in the acquirement of useful information concerning any object, is, to clearly identify that object with its name. It has been the special object of the writer to convey, by the simplest means—literary and pictorial—an accurate knowledge of the various Trees and Shrubs indigenous to Britain, as well as of their uses, beauties, and attributes; and in order to enhance the interest of the subject, he has added notes on some of the animal inhabitants and insect tribes, whose history is often most intimately connected with that of the plants they attach themselves to.

A few trees have also been introduced which, though really of foreign origin, have become so thoroughly naturalized on our soil, and from their character are so identified in our minds as native productions, as to rank harmoniously with the older denizens of English forests and woodlands.

LONDON, *April*, 1859.

CONTENTS.

	PAGE
INTRODUCTORY	1
THE OAK	5
THE BEECH.—(*Fagus sylvaticus*)	21
THE HORNBEAM.—(*Carpinus Betulus*)	27
THE ASH.—(*Fraxinus excelsior*)	29
THE ELM.—(*Ulmus campestris*)	34
THE WYCH ELM, OR SCOTCH ELM.—(*Ulmus montana*)	39
THE BIRCH.—(*Betula alba*)	41
THE DWARF BIRCH.—(*Betula nána*)	46
THE SCOTCH PINE OR FIR.—(*Pinus sylvéstris*)	47
THE LARCH.—(*Lárix Europǽa*)	52
THE FIELD MAPLE.—(*A'cer campéstre*)	54
THE SYCAMORE.—(*A'cer Pséudo-plátanus*)	56
THE LIME-TREE, OR LINDEN.—(*Tília Europǽa*)	59
THE WALNUT.—(*Júglans régia*)	63
THE EATABLE OR SPANISH CHESTNUT.—(*Castánea vésca*)	66
THE HORSE CHESTNUT.—(*Æ'sculus Hippocástanum*)	69
THE WILD PEAR TREE.—(*Pyrus commúnis*)	72
THE WILD APPLE OR CRAB-TREE.—(*Pyrus Málus*)	73
THE WILD SERVICE TREE.—(*Pyrus torminális*)	77
THE WHITE BEAM TREE.—(*Pyrus Aria*)	78
THE MOUNTAIN ASH, OR ROAN TREE.—(*Pyrus Aucupária*)	80
THE MEDLAR.—(*Méspilus germánica*)	82
THE ALDER.—(*A'lnus glutinósa*)	84
THE WILLOW	86
THE COMMON WHITE WILLOW.—(*Sálix álba*)	88
THE GOAT-WILLOW, OR SAUGH.—(*Sálix cáprea*)	93
THE COMMON OSIER.—(*Sálix viminális*)	97
THE WHITE POPLAR OR ABELE TREE.—(*Pópulus álba*)	99
THE ASPEN, OR TREMBLING POPLAR.—(*Pópulus trémula*)	103
THE BLACK POPLAR.—(*Pópulus nígra*)	105
THE LOMBARDY POPLAR.—(*Pópulus fastigiáta*)	107
THE YEW.—(*Táxus baccáta*)	108
THE MISTLETOE.—(*Víscum álbum*)	113
THE IVY.—(*Hédera Hélix*)	115
THE ARBUTUS, OR STRAWBERRY-TREE.—(*A'rbutus unédo*)	118

CONTENTS.

	PAGE
THE HEATH-LANDS	119
THE FURZE, OR GORSE.—(*Ulex Európæ us*)	124
THE BILBERRY.—(*Vaccínium Myrtíllus*)	126
THE BLEABERRY, OR BOG WHORTLEBERRY.—(*Vaccínium uliginósum*)	129
THE COWBERRY, OR MOUNT IDA WHORTLEBERRY.—(*Vaccínium Vítis Idæ'a*)	130
THE CRANBERRY.—(*Oxycóccus palústris*)	132
THE COMMON BEARBERRY.—(*Arctostáphylos Uva-Ursi*)	134
THE BLACK CROWBERRY.—(*Empétrum nigrum*)	136
THE COMMON JUNIPER.—(*Juníperus commúnis*)	137
THE BOX.—(*Búxus sempervírens*)	139
THE SWEET GALE, OR CANDLEBERRY MYRTLE.—(*Myríca Gále*)	140
THE LEAST WILLOW.—(*Sálix herbácea*)	142
THE CLOUD-BERRY.—(*Rúbus Chamæmórus*)	143
THE STONE BRAMBLE.—(*Rúbus saxátilis*)	145
THE WILD RASPBERRY.—(*Rúbus idæus*)	145
THE DEWBERRY, OR GREY BRAMBLE.—(*Rúbus cæ'sius*)	147
THE COMMON BLACKBERRY, OR BRAMBLE.—(*Rúbus fruticósus*)	148
THE HEDGES	151
THE HAWTHORN, OR WHITETHORN.—(*Cratægus Oxyacantha*)	153
THE HOLLY.—(*Ilex Aquifolium*)	155
THE HAZEL.—(*Córylus Avellána*)	158
THE BIRD CHERRY.—(*Prúnus Pádus*)	161
THE SLOE, OR BLACKTHORN.—(*Prúnus spinósa*)	162
THE BARBERRY.—(*Bérberis vulgáris*)	165
THE GUELDER ROSE.—(*Vibúrnum Opulus*)	167
THE WAYFARING TREE.—(*Vibúrnum Lantána*)	168
THE BUCKTHORN.—(*Rhámnus cathárticus*)	169
THE SEA BUCKTHORN, OR SALLOW THORN.—(*Hippóphäe rhamnóides*)	170
THE DOGWOOD, OR WILD CORNEL.—(*Córnus sanguínea*)	172
THE SPINDLE-TREE.—(*Euónymus európæ'us*)	173
THE ELDER.—(*Sambúcus nigra*)	175
WILD ROSES	177
THE WOODBINE, OR COMMON HONEYSUCKLE.—(*Lonicéra Periclymenum*)	180
THE PERFOLIATE HONEYSUCKLE.—(*Lonicéra Caprifólium*)	181
WILD CURRANTS AND GOOSEBERRIES.—(*Genus Ribes*)	182
THE PRIVET.—(*Ligustrum vulgáre*)	183
THE BUTCHER'S BROOM.—(*Rúscus aculeátus*)	184
APPENDIX	187

OUR WOODLANDS,
HEATHS, AND HEDGES.

INTRODUCTORY.

Before we proceed to describe in detail the subject-matter of the following pages, we think it desirable to offer some brief preliminary remarks applicable to the subject in general.

To begin with definitions. *Trees*, and their lesser relatives, *shrubs*, are defined to be, plants possessed of a firm, *woody* stem, divided at a certain height into branches, which terminate in leaves; while *herbaceous* plants, in contradistinction to these, have all the parts of a fleshy texture, and are destitute of woody stems. Such a plant, for example, is the Primrose, in common with the majority of our wild flowers. The further distinction between a tree and a shrub is a somewhat arbitrary one, depending only on their relative size; or, in other words, a shrub is merely a tree of humbler growth; and, indeed, we find that frequently a plant that takes the form of a shrub in one locality, rises into the dimensions of a tree when placed under more favouring circumstances of soil and atmosphere.

Trees are not only the grandest of vegetable productions, but they far exceed all other organized structures, animal or vegetable, in magnitude and in longevity; while their vast and essential importance to the well-being of man, and the beauty of the earth, can only be estimated in some degree by mentally comparing the aspect and condition of a treeless world with that we now enjoy, so bounteously furnished by Providence with these objects of greatest ornament and utility. Without the aid of timber, the arts and manufactures of civilized life could hardly have progressed to any satisfactory extent. Our architecture, our ships, machinery, furniture, agricultural implements, &c., all owe their very existence to that of trees.

Again, in the absence of trees, where would be the charm of landscape scenery, the tufted hill-side, the tree-embosomed lake, the forest-glade, and all the thousand delights of country life, which are so intimately associated with the presence of trees? But we need not further enlarge on these considerations, which are patent to the feelings of every one of us.

We must, however, mention one peculiar advantage

which trees possess, as landscape ornaments, over the more evanescent herbaceous plants, and that is, their constant, yet changeful beauty in every season of the year; a quality especially observable in those large assemblies of various trees, called forests, where the charm of wild sylvan Nature reigns paramount. Lovely are the woodlands in fresh early Spring, when bright buds of tenderest verdure are put forth, to the song of the feathered choir, whose nests are rocked in many a leafy bough.—Deeply beautiful are they in full Summer, with their cool and welcome shade, the hum of many insects, and that sweet airy music produced by the rustling branches. Then, as the golden Autumn steals over the forest, comes the period of its richest glory;— that in which the painter revels, vainly tasking his palette for its imitation : and though these bright hues are the tokens of decay, the foliage has a glory in its approaching dissolution, unknown to it in youth and vigour.

> "Those virgin leaves, of purest vivid green,
> Which charm'd ere yet they trembled on the trees,
> Now cheer the sober landscape in decay :
> The lime first fading; and the golden birch,
> With bark of silver hue; the moss-grown oak,
> Tenacious of its leaves of russet brown;
> The ensanguined dog-wood; and a thousand tints,
> Which Flora dress'd in all her pride of bloom
> Could scarcely equal, decorate the groves."

The leaves fall; tender plants wither and wholly

disappear; and Winter comes: but even he fails to rob the forest trees of their grandeur, and of all their graces also; while the advent of snow re-invests each twig and branch with a strange fantastic array, emulating in beauty with their summer vesture.

It will be unnecessary here to enter into a description of the organization, growth, &c. of trees, which are similar in those respects to other plants; this it is the province of Botany to elucidate; and we must therefore refer the reader, desirous of becoming acquainted with the general phenomena of vegetable life, and the various structures concerned in it, to one of the numerous popular works on that interesting science.

We have, however, considered it desirable, for the benefit of those readers who have mastered the terms used in botanical description, to give, in the form of foot-notes, the generic and specific characters of each plant, framed in accordance with those made use of in Loudon's "Encyclopædia" of Plants.

We would here cordially recommend to the reader a work called "Wild Flowers, and how to gather them," by Spencer Thompson, M.D. &c.; in the first part of which will be found an excellent introduction to the structure and functions of the different organs of a plant, with an explanation of the technical terms used in Botany.

THE OAK.

At the head of our indigenous trees—hallowed by innumerable associations and traditions—stands the majestic Oak, the Monarch of the Forest. But, before we proceed to expatiate upon its varied claims to our admiration and fond regard, we must first give a brief account of its botanical character.

It will be noticed that in Plate A, two forms of the Oak are figured, in one of which the acorns are supported on long footstalks, while in the other they are directly seated, or as it is termed, "sessile," upon the branch; there are also some few other unimportant distictions between the two, which have led modern botanists to regard them as two distinct species, to which they have given the scientific names of *Quercus pedunculata*,[1] the Peduncled Oak (Plate A, fig. 1), and *Quercus sessiliflora*,[2] the Sessile-fruited Oak (Plate A,

---

[1] *Quercus pedunculata.* Nat. order, *Corylaceæ;* Lin. Syst. *Monœcia Polyandria.* Gen. char.: Barren flower in a lax catkin; perianth, single, somewhat 5-cleft; stamens, 5 to 10. Fertile flower, involucre, cup-shaped, scaly; perianth, single, incorporated with the germen, 6-lobed; germen 3-celled, 2 of them abortive, style 1, stigmas 3.—Spec. char.: Leaves oblong, subsessile, smooth, sinuated; lobes, round; fruit, oblong, stalked.

[2] *Q. sessiliflora.* Spec. char.: Leaves deciduous, oblong, smooth, dilated upwards, stalked; lobes, obtuse; stalks of fruit elongated; nut, oblong.

fig. 2), and to lend countenance to this distinction, it was supposed that the timber of the sessile-fruited kind was much inferior to that of the common or peduncled Oak for ship-building and other purposes, but recent experiments have proved pretty satisfactorily that there is but little to choose between the two ; the former in some cases excelling the latter, and *vice versâ*, according to the more or less favourable nature of the soil on which the respective trees had been grown.

As the differences, therefore, whether sufficiently marked to constitute distinct species, or merely varieties, are practically so unimportant, and, as the history and statistics of the two trees are almost identical, we prefer to simplify the matter by generally speaking of them indiscriminately as *the* Oak, though we shall nevertheless figure the two forms for those who wish for a more exact knowledge of the subject.

The peduncled Oak is generally the most abundant of the two kinds, but it has been remarked that in some few parts of the country the sessile-fruited tree prevails almost exclusively.

The growth of the Oak is slower than that of any other native forest tree, and it requires several centuries to attain its full grandeur. The Great Oak at Panshanger, for instance, one of the most magnificent trees in the country, is more than 250 years old, but has still all the vigour and beauty of a young tree, and may be considered as yet in its prime, although a century ago, it was called the Great Oak.

The young trees usually first produce acorns when about fifteen to eighteen years old, though in some cases it occurs earlier than this. These acorns, or "oak-mast," as they are collectively called, are not now regarded of the same importance that they were in days of yore, the demand for them being chiefly confined to the small number required to insure a future supply of trees. Time was, when our remote and rough progenitors had little better fare to look to in the way of daily bread than this kindly largess of the Oak; and this, moreover, with no great detriment to their health and longevity, if we are to credit the flattering report of the poet, who speaks of men that

> "Fed with the Oaken mast,
> The aged trees themselves in age surpassed."

The name 'acorn' itself seems to point to its use as a substitute for the cereals, 'Ac' being the Saxon original of the word 'Oak;' so that acorn is simply 'oak-corn.'

As civilization advanced, however, this simple aliment was almost entirely abandoned by man in favour of wheat and other varieties of food, while swine took his place in the woods, and to them the acorn crop, except in times of famine, has for ages past been resigned. In the records of early English history frequent reference is made to the feeding of swine in the woods, under the name of "pannage," oaks in those days, being principally valued on account of the food they afforded. Evelyn says, in reference to their use in this respect, that "a peck of acorns a day, with a little bran, will make a hog increase a pound weight per diem for two months together."

It is evident from history that the surface of Britain was formerly far more covered with oak-forests than at present; and the names of towns and other places derived from this tree are extremely numerous, much exceeding those associated by name with any other; although the beech, ash, and elm lay claim to a similar distinction. But we must bear in mind that our present orthography of O-a-k was not always that adopted by our ancestors for this tree, the original Saxon being, as above-mentioned, Ac; then through a series of variations, ack, oc, oxe, auck, uck, hoke, and divers other contortions; thus *a w* was tacked on at the beginning making it *wok*, &c., much in the same way as, in some parts of the country, we may still hear the rustic speak of oats as "wuts."

With this explanation very many names may be recognised as having been derived from this national tree, even when the actual word "Oak" does not at all appear. The London suburb of *Ac*ton is equivalent to Oak-town; *A*crington, Oakring-town; *Wock-*

ham, *Hok*enorton and a host of others might be adduced as associated in one way or another with the Oak.

The use of oak timber for maritime and domestic purposes is coeval in this country with the growth of civilization. The Ancient Britons indeed appear to have possessed some sort of an oak-built navy from the earliest periods of their history; when they were content to live ashore without houses but in caves; and so efficient were they that the Romans complained a good deal of the toughness of our ships' sides, on which the "beaks" of their war galleys could make but little impression.[1]

Passing to later times, we find the timber of the Oak becomes an object of paramount value and importance, identifying itself with Britain's naval and mercantile greatness.

> "Let India boast her plants, nor envy we
> The weeping amber and the balmy tree;
> While by our *Oaks* the precious loads are borne,
> And realms commanded which those trees adorn."
> POPE.

The same qualities of surpassing strength and durability, which led to the employment of oak in shipbuilding, naturally recommended its use in sacred and

---

[1] The name of our island in the ancient British tongue was "Clas Merddin,"—"The sea-defended green spot," a title beautiful and appropriate, from that time to this.

domestic architecture; and accordingly, in all our oldest cathedrals, churches, and other edifices, we meet with examples of oak, often of equal antiquity with the building itself, and yet as strong and sound at heart as when placed there centuries ago. As a familiar instance we may mention the carved oaken shrine of Edward the Confessor, in Westminster Abbey, executed some 800 years since. At Winchester, in St. Stephen's Chapel, is preserved as one of the chief curiosities of the place, a circular table of oak, eighteen feet across, and all in one entire piece; being, in fact, a transverse slice from the trunk of an immense tree. This is actually believed, by many, to be the real old "King Arthur's Round Table," so famous in history and, if we may credit such a notion, here is to be seen a piece of oak furniture 1,300 years old. At any rate, there is abundant and direct evidence that it has been in the place where it now is for 700 years; an age sufficient to entitle it to be regarded as a most precious and venerable relic.

At Greenstead, near Ongar, in Essex, there is a very curious old wooden church, the walls of which are framed of oak trunks split through the centre, and roughly pegged together. This church is believed to have been hastily put up, more than 900 years ago, as a temporary *sanctum* for the body of St. Edmund (slain A.D. 946), and afterwards converted into a parish church, with some slight additions and alterations. The original timbers, after this immense lapse of time, are still sound internally, and may probably last yet as long a time as they have done already.

The timber in many old buildings, which till lately had always been considered to be chestnut, has been proved to be that of the sessile-fruited Oak, which has more of what is called technically the "flash," or silver grain, and has altogether a paler appearance than that of the commoner, or peduncled kind.

Of all organized objects in creation, whether animal or vegetable, a tree has by far the longest existence, and, among English trees, the Oak exceeds all others in longevity;[1] so that Dryden has rather under, than over estimated its duration, in those fine lines describing the course of an old Oak:—

> "The monarch Oak, the patriarch of trees,
> Shoots rising up, and spreads by slow degrees;
> Three centuries he grows, and three he stays,
> Supreme in state, and in three more decays."

Throughout our land, there is hardly a district that is without its oaks, remarkable for their immense age, size, or legendary and historical associations. Of these, we could, did space permit, give a copious list; but must be content with selecting a few of the more notable examples.

[1] Possibly excepting the Yew, which is known sometimes to attain to a vast age.

One of the grandest and oldest of these is the Cowthorpe Oak, standing on the banks of the river Nidd, in Yorkshire, which, close to the ground, measures seventy-eight feet in circumference; one of the branches of this tree, blown off in a gale of wind, contained upwards of five tons of wood. In Norfolk is the Winfarthing Oak, said to have been an old tree at the time of the Conquest, though its exact age is unknown. The circumference of the trunk is seventy feet, and within its hollow stem there is room sufficient to accommodate thirty persons. The Merton Oak, on Lord Walsingham's estate, in the same county, has also an enormous trunk, sixty-three feet in circumference. The Salcey-forest Oak in Northamptonshire, is supposed, on good grounds, to be more than 1,500 years old, and is described by Sir T. D. Lauder as "one of the most picturesque sylvan ruins that can be met with anywhere." Though much decayed and wasted it still produces an annual crop of leaves and acorns.

In Nannau Park, near Dolgelly, North Wales, there stood an immense Oak (twenty-seven feet in girth) which had for centuries been celebrated among the Welsh, by the various names of the "Hobgoblin's Hollow-Tree," the "Haunted Oak," the "Spirit-Blasted Tree;" and there is a weird tradition concerning it, that Howel Sele, a Welsh chieftain, and once Lord of Nannau, was killed in a hunting quarrel by his cousin Owen Glendower and his friend Madoc, none others being near to see the deed. But before life was yet extinct, the murderers bore the body of the unfortunate Howel to this tree, and hid it in the hollow trunk. Glendower hastened to his stronghold, Glendewrdry, and the friends of Howel, alarmed at his non-appearance, sought long but vainly for him; and though it is said that groans and hollow sounds were heard by those who wandered near the tree, none bethought themselves to look within the trunk. So years passed by; the old Oak preserved the bloody trust confided to it, till at last a time came when the cruel Owen Glendower found himself on his death-bed, and unwilling that his dread secret should survive him, he extorted a promise from Madoc, his accomplice, to divulge the truth. Madoc kept his word, search was made in the spot indicated, and in the hollow of the tree appeared the skeleton of Howel, in an upright posture, and grasping with bony hand his rusted sword. The remains of Howel were thereupon removed to the neighbouring monastery of Cymmer for interment, and masses were performed for the repose of his troubled spirit. So runs the legend, and the Haunted Oak was pointed at for 400 years after the discovery of its sepulchral character, till in 1813 it was blown down, and its wood, very dark and beautiful, was manufactured into a variety of objects to gratify the curious in such relics.

The Cadenham Oak, in the New Forest, about two miles from Lyndhurst, is less remarkable for its age than for its curious property of putting forth annually a few leaves at Christmas-time.

In Clipstone Park, Nottinghamshire, stands a venerable tree, called the Parliament Oak, from a tradition that under its branches a parliament was held by Edward the First in the year 1290 ; and it is probable that it was, even at that remote time, an old and large tree.

In these grand *living* monuments of the past there is a peculiar interest, which attaches to no other object, and which serves to intensify our attachment to the time-honoured country of our birth ; for we are conscious, when looking at one of these, that we are in the presence of that selfsame life, which began, it may be, in Saxon times, a thousand years ago,—and now, while generation after generation of human beings, as well as of other creatures, have lived and died around it, while dynasty after dynasty has risen and fallen, great revolutions have occurred, and new worlds have been discovered,—there it stands, the same majestic, brave old Oak, clothing with yearly verdure the same branches which canopied, perchance, not only monarchs, but still greater men in days of yore.

As to the picturesque attributes of the Oak, every lover of nature and student of art will appreciate its high value as a component part of landscape scenery, whether regarded in the rich beauty of its prime, or in the gnarled majesty of its old age and decay,—and this, independently of those associations which have rendered the Oak pre-eminently the tree of the poet and of the historian. In every natural situation the presence of the Oak is welcome, and sure to heighten the interest of the scene. As Gilpin, in his eloquent eulogy of the Oak observes: "It adds new dignity to the ruined tower and the Gothic arch; by stretching its wild moss-grown branches athwart their weird walls, it gives them a kind of majesty coeval with itself; at the same time, its propriety is still preserved if it throws its arms over the purling brook or the mantling pool, where it beholds

'Its reverend image in the expanse below.'"

And winter, even, does not divest it of its grandeur, for then its massive trunk, and the grim contortions of its Herculean limbs are displayed with startling effect. Truly, the Oak is the King of our Forests.

The superstitions and legends investing the Oak—handed down from the earliest ages of all nations among whom it grows—can only be glanced at here. The Greeks fabled that Jupiter took this tree under his protection, giving the Oaks of Dodona the power of augury, and thus making them "talking Oaks." From its leaves were wreathed the civic crowns of the Romans, and the mysteries of Druidism were performed under groves of this venerated tree.

> "The sacred Oaks,
> Among whose awful shades the Druids strayed,
> To cut the hallow'd mistletoe, and hold
> High converse with their gods."

The poetry of our country abounds in allusions to this tree, but, we think, the finest poem wholly addressed to it is Cowper's "Yardley Oak."

Of the medicinal properties of the Oak, otherwise than as a simple astringent, there is little to say, notwithstanding the list of virtues attributed to it by our forefathers, and enumerated by Evelyn in his "Sylva;" and the assertion gravely made by one Paulus, a Danish physician, we venture to disbelieve, that "a handful or two of small oak-buttons mingled with oats and given to horses which are black, will, in a few days eating, alter their colour to a fine dapple grey; and this because of the vitriol abounding in the tree." A decoction of oak-*bark* has, however, been sometimes used in modern medicine, but more powerful astringents imported from abroad, such as Peruvian-bark, &c., are generally preferred to it.

It remains yet to speak of that teeming insect population of the Oak, the immense variety of which renders it a perfect treasury to the naturalist, and whose history

THE OAK.

would of itself fill a volume ; for no portion of the tree is exempt from the tax which these little tribes lay upon it. Of this host, the greater number find food and shelter in the foliage, but some eat into the wood itself, while others carry on mining operations in and under the bark, which they drill in all directions. Altogether, no less than some 1,500 species of insects have been described as subsisting on the Oak ; and about 500 more being attached to these as parasites, it brings the whole number to about 2,000 different species, all depending, directly or indirectly, on the Oak for support. We do not, of course, mean to say that all this assembly is to be found upon a single tree, or at one season ; but a very considerable number of kinds will reward the search of the naturalist during every month of the year, the summer and autumnal months being, as might be supposed, the most productive.

That glory of butterfly collectors, the Purple Emperor, is celebrated for his attachment to the Oak, enthroning himself on the loftiest branch, from which ever and anon he takes that lordly flight, that so often tantalizes the eager entomologist, who has small chances of securing the prize, unless armed with a net on a pole some thirty feet long. But the only butterfly that really *feeds* on the Oak is the Purple Hair-streak, a very lively and beautiful little insect, whose sports on and around the tree we have watched with great pleasure and amusement. Three or four of these little butterflies often engage together in a series of rapid evolutions— half sportive, half pugnacious—the purple of their wings glittering beautifully as they dart in and out among the foliage.

PURPLE EMPEROR AND PURPLE HAIR-STREAK BUTTERFLIES.

Of moths, a great host inhabit the tree, including many of our finest kinds, such as the Goat Moth and Wood-leopard Moth, the caterpillars of which consume the solid wood, boring long galleries through the trunk; others feed on the leaves, in the larva state: among these the Oak Egger, the Emperor, the Buff-tip, the Lobster, the Merveil du Jour, the Red Underwings, the Oak Beauty, and divers other beautiful species.

There is a large section of diminutive moths, whose habits form a very interesting study for the naturalist, as they adopt varied and curious modes of protecting themselves while feeding and undergoing their transformations. Some joining several leaves together by means of silken threads, so as to form a hollow case, in which the creature dwells; others attain the like object by rolling up a single leaf: this is done by the very common and beautiful little green Oak Moth.[1]

Others, again, feed on the inner substance of the leaf, inserting themselves between the upper and lower membranes, which they leave uninjured; this produces those bladdery-looking blotches often seen on the Oak-leaf.

Several of our largest beetles also feed on the Oak, some on the wood, and others on the leaves; among the latter is the common Cockchafer, which is often a terrible enemy to this tree, whole forests of it having been stripped of their foliage by this devastating insect. The giant Stag-beetle feeds upon the rotten wood found in hollow stumps of oak. Those singular productions called "galls" are more numerous on this than on any other tree. They are to be found in diversified forms on the dead branches and flower-stalks; these originate in the puncture of minute insects called Gall-flies (*Cynips*), and are designed for the protection of their tender offspring. Oak-apples, so much in vogue on the

"Twenty-ninth of May,
Oak-Apple Day,"

---

[1] Figured and described in "The Common Objects of the Country," by Rev. J. G. Wood; as also, is the Emperor Moth, and some others of the Oak-feeding insects.

are also excrescences of this nature, as are the galls used for dyeing and ink-making, which are largely imported from abroad,—but these are the produce of another species of oak; those found in this country, however, possess nearly the same properties. The pretty "Oak-spangles," which stud the under side of the leaves, were formerly considered to be parasitic fungi, but are now ascertained to be the work of gall-flies, as also are those currant-like little spheres attached to the flower-stalk. But want of space compels us to abbreviate this subject, and we must altogether omit describing in detail the numerous tribes of plants which are parasitic on the Oak, consisting of mosses, lichens, and fungi. The mistletoe, though occasionally found on the Oak, is far more frequent on other trees, and will have a separate notice.

THE BEECH.—(*Fagus sylvaticus.*)

WELL do we remember how, in our school-boy days, when first set down to puzzle out the Pastorals of Virgil, our imagination dwelt on the tantalizing allusion to "beechen-shades," in the well-known,

"Tityre, tu patulæ recubans sub tegmine fagi,"

till we would almost have exchanged persons with even an "old classical party" like Tityrus, to be in the beechwoods too, instead of that hot, close school-room; with a mossy turf beneath, and the flickering green leaves, the squirrel, and the birds above us, in lieu of the hard "form" and low cracked ceiling that were our seat and canopy.

Thus mentally wandering in woodland dreams—our real bucolic business has eke been forgotten—till, instead of awaking to find ourselves under beechen boughs,

LEAF AND FRUIT OF BEECH.

[1] *Fagus sylvatica.* Nat. order, *Corylaceæ ;* Lin. syst. *Monœcia Polyandria. Gen. char.*: Barren flower in a globose catkin; perianth, single, of 1 leaf, campanulate, 6-cleft; stamens, 5 to 12. Fertile flower 2, within a 4-lobed prickly involucre; perianth, single, urceolate, with 4-5 minute lobes; germen, incorporated with the perianth, 3-celled, two of them becoming abortive; styles 3; nuts 1 seeded, invested with the enlarged

we were, perchance, aroused to duty by the twigs of a less pleasant tree, to wit, "the birch," waving over us with a dismal hiss.

Among our truly indigenous forest-trees, the Beech must certainly rank as second only to the oak, for majesty and picturesqueness; while, for the union of grace and nobility, it may claim precedence over every other member of our Sylva.[1]

Having said this, we must, as a matter of course, dissent from the opinion of Gilpin, the highly gifted author of "Forest Scenery," who has, and as we think, unjustly, impugned the ornamental character of this generally favourite tree; and this, because he had some crotchets of his own about landscape composition, and the shape that trees *ought* to take to make them good subjects for the pencil. The Beech did not happen to fit itself to his theory, so he quarrelled with it, and called it hard names. The most beautiful tree-portrait we ever remember to have seen was that of a Beech exhibited a season or two ago at one of the Water-colour Societies, and we are sure that no one looking at this, could allow, with Gilpin, that the Beech was not admirable in a picture.

involucre.— Spec. char.: Leaves ovate, glabrous, obsoletely dentate, their margins ciliated.

[1] The Sweet Chestnut can hardly be called with propriety a native forest-tree; otherwise it would at least divide the honours with the Beech.

THE BEECH.

The autumnal hues of the Beech are rich and glowing in the extreme ; and when a beech-grove has assumed the intense orange yellow which it displays at a certain season, the effect is most striking ; the radiance overhead being repeated by the fallen leaves below, till earth and air seem saturated with golden light.

There is great picturesque beauty in the trunk of an old Beech, generally fantastic in form, with all sorts of hollows and knobs, often with the semblance of clustered columns, giving a fine Gothic effect ; but the great charm of this part of the tree lies in the smooth olive-grey bark painted and gilded with various-tinted lichens, and embossed with large patches of dark velvet-green moss, which spreads most luxuriantly over the high-growing roots, and renders them the most tempting of rustic seats.

This bark, too, from its smooth and tender surface, especially invites the wandering lover to carve thereon the name he adores ; and thus we often find a noble beech-trunk, profusely "illustrated with cuts," in that well-known style of art which has been in vogue from the earliest times with the victims of sentiment, including Shakspeare's Orlando, the culprit referred to in the speech of Rosalind :

"There is a man haunts the forest, that abuses our young trees with carving *Rosalind* on their barks."

There is an extraordinary variety of the Beech called the Purple Beech, now become pretty frequent in parks and pleasure grounds, which has its leaves, when quite young, of a cherry-red colour; and at midsummer, when quite matured, of such an intense purple, as to look almost black; producing a strange, and yet pleasing effect, when seen at a distance, in combination with the green of other trees, to which it acts as a foil.

The original tree, from which all the Purple Beeches in Europe have been derived, was found by accident in a wood in Germany about ninety years ago, but what gave rise to such a remarkable and permanent deviation from the ordinary colour of the foliage, it is impossible to say.

The Copper-coloured Beech, often seen with the last, is merely a sub-variety, with the purple element less developed.

The fruit of the Beech, called "beech-mast," is a bristly capsule (as shown in the figure above), containing two sharp cornered triangular nuts, which, falling from the husk in October and November, may then be found scattered on the ground beneath. The kernel resembles the hazel-nut in its pleasant flavour, and is considered to be of very wholesome quality; but as an article of utility, beech-mast is generally neglected in this country; a few pigs and poultry only being sent into the woods to feed and fatten on it. On

THE BEECH.

the Continent, however, large quantities of oil, excellent both for burning and culinary purposes, are extracted from the kernels, which in some districts thus become an important source of profit to the inhabitants.

The wood of this tree is very hard, close-grained, and rather brittle, but is used for an immense variety of purposes which we have not space to enumerate. We may remark, however, that a large proportion of the common stained and japanned furniture used in modern dwellings is manufactured from Beech. It is also a favourite wood for fuel, especially in Paris, where it is consumed to an immense extent under the name of *bois d'Andelle.*

The Beech, growing in a favourable situation, will often attain to dimensions rivalling those of the largest oaks. There is one of extreme antiquity and vast size standing on Sunning Hill, in Windsor Forest, which measures (at six feet from the ground) thirty-six feet in circumference. In general, a full-grown Beech varies in height from sixty to one hundred feet, though there are many in the kingdom that considerably exceed the latter altitude.

In comparison with the myriad insects that resort to the oak, those of the Beech are far from numerous, but a few caterpillars of our finest moths are found to be feeders on the foliage. The most curious of these is that of the

Lobster Moth, a grotesque, nondescript-looking creature, very dissimilar to any other caterpillar found in this country, as it has long spider-like fore-legs, and two tail-like appendages behind, so that altogether it has no very distant resemblance to a lobster, whence its name. The moth, however, into which this odd creature is eventually transformed has nothing remarkable in its appearance.

Notwithstanding the paucity of insects actually feeding on this tree, many species take refuge in its umbrageous foliage, from which they may be shaken out and captured; and the naturalist who spends a day in the woods where the Beech is abundant will not lack occupation and interest, for there are many plants especially alluring to insects, that are generally associated with Beech trees. The fungi also of Beech woods are numerous, and highly interesting; among them being the Truffle, precious to epicures, and the almost equally esteemed Morel, besides many species remarkable for their beauty, one of which, found growing on the trunks of Beech-trees in the autumn, is like a tuft of white feathery coral,[1] and possesses the recommendation of being esculent; though we would advise our readers not to experiment on the gastronomic qualities of fungi without the guidance of a trustworthy book on the subject, to insure their getting hold of the right

[1] Hydnum Coralloides.

species, as some of the most deadly varieties have a considerable general resemblance to the most wholesome kinds.

THE HORNBEAM.[1]—(*Carpinus Betulus.*)

WE place the Hornbeam next to the Beech, as it is often mistaken for that tree, to which, indeed, it bears so great a general resemblance as hardly to be distinguishable at a first glance, except that the leaves are wanting in that glossy varnish which marks those of the Beech, and on closer examination will be seen to have a very different form and texture, being doubly toothed at the edges, with deeply marked parallel ribs, and rough surface; but the young, half-expanded leaves are very lovely, of a delicate green, and most beautifully folded or crimped longitudinally. The Hornbeam is very common in many parts of the country, but especially

[1] *Carpinus Betulus.* Nat. order, *Corylaceæ;* Lin. syst. *Monœcia Polyandria.* Gen. char.: Barren flower in a cylindrical catkin, its scales roundish, ciliated at the base; stamens, 8 to 20. Fertile flower, in a lax catkin, its scales large, foliaceous, 3-lobed, 1 flowered, involucre 0; perianth of 1 leaf, urceolate, 6-dentate, incorporated with the 2-celled germen, of which one cell is abortive; styles 2; nut ovate, striated, 1-seeded.—Spec. char.: scales or bractas of the fruit oblong, serrated with two smaller lateral lobes.

abounds in Essex, where it constitutes the principal tree of Epping and Hainault forests. As we generally see it, it has the form of a low tree or hedge shrub, having been reduced to this state by repeated clipping; but when allowed its free growth it attains a good height, sometimes as much as forty or fifty feet, with a trunk two feet in thickness. But though it then has much of the character of the Beech, it is deficient in the picturesque beauty of the latter, being too "lumpy," or as it is termed "cabbage-headed," in form.

LEAF AND CATKIN OF HORNBEAM.

The chief recommendation of the Hornbeam, at the present day, is the value of its timber, which is particularly hard and tough, and excellent for the cogs of mill-wheels, and is otherwise much used in the manufacture of agricultural implements. The yokes of oxen from time immemorial have been made of this wood. But in the days of geometric gardening, it was a favourite tree for the close-trimmed hedges, and clipped screens, which served to partition the formal alleys and flower-beds, then considered essential to a well-ordered pleasure-garden; and it certainly makes admirable hedges for such purposes, especially as the brown withered leaves remain till they are supplanted by new ones, affording an excellent protection to more tender plants.

The Hornbeam has also been called Horse-beech, Hard-beam Yoke Elm, and Witch-Hazel.

The foliage is not much attacked by insects, but the caterpillars of several moths feed upon it.

THE ASH.—(*Fraxinus excelsior.*)

"Fraxinus in Sylvis pulcherrima." VIRGIL.

WHILE the oak has been justly called the Hercules of the forest, the Ash has equally merited the title of the Sylvan Venus, from the elegance of its form, the feathery lightness of its foliage, and the graceful waving of its branches—qualities especially to be appreciated

[1] *Fraxinus excelsior.* Nat. order, Oleaceæ; Lin. syst. *Diandria Monogynia.* Gen. char : Calyx none, or in 4 segments; corolla none, or in 4 linear segments; germen superior, 2-celled; capsule with 1 or 2 seeds, leaf like; seeds pendulous, some flowers without anthers.—Spec. char. : Leaflets serrated; flowers without calyx or corolla.

when it is grouped with other trees of more massive character, or, as we have frequently seen and admired it, growing, as it loves to do, by brook or river side, with an accompaniment of grey rocks, whose heavy forms and sombre hue give full effect to the airiness and fresh verdure of the Ash.

Nor is it always inferior to the oak and beech in height and extent of branch. There is a magnificent Ash-tree in Woburn Park, probably the largest in England, being 90 feet high, and the trunk of which measures more than 20 feet round; the whole tree contains 872 feet of solid timber. There are, however, many others in the kingdom which approach this in magnitude. In Ireland, at Donirey, near Clare, is a hollow trunk of one which is forty-two feet in circumference.

BUD, LEAF, AND SEED OF ASH.

Next to the oak, the Ash is, doubtless, the most useful timber tree we possess, being used for innumerable purposes where toughness and elasticity are desirable. To the wheelwright, and agricultural implement maker, it is invaluable; while its lightness, combined with strength, renders it generally the best material for boat-oars, handles of spades and axes, not forgetting the tourist's *Alpen-stock*, &c.

Ordinary Ash-timber cannot be considered as ornamental or fit for the cabinet-maker's purposes; but the roots are often very curiously veined, as are the warty excrescences on the trunk, and are admirable for fine cabinet-work.

This tree has been the object of some curious superstitions; one of which at least, absurd as it is, is not yet quite obsolete:—we allude to the reputed virtue of a split Ash-tree in curing ruptured children. The programme of the ceremony by which this supposed power was called into play is as follows:—The stem of a young Ash being cleft down the middle, and kept open by wedges, the afflicted child, in a state of nudity, was forced through the opening; the mother standing on one side of the tree, and the father on the other. This uncomfortable transit having been twice performed by the astonished and shivering infant, both it and the disrupted tree were respectively swathed up at the same time; and if the wound in the latter healed and the parts coalesced, as was generally the case, a simultaneous cure was supposed to be effected in the child.

It is but a short time ago, that a poor child, suffering from the above infirmity, was actually subjected to this process somewhere in Warwickshire.

In many parts of the country we meet with old Ash-trees bearing deep scars or seams down their sides; memorials of the ill usage they were subjected to in their youth, from the gross ignorance of the peasantry, for the benefit of suffering babes.

Equally celebrated and unfounded were the potent curative virtues of the contrivance known as a Shrew-Ash. There is a gentle, harmless little creature, with a long nose, called a "shrew-mouse," which, however, our sagacious forefathers invested with a terribly malignant character, insisting it was of so venomous a nature that whenever it happened to creep over the limb of a cow, horse, or sheep, that limb would be forthwith seized with grievous pains and loss of power. To provide against such an accident, always liable to occur, the good folks set their fancy to work, and composed an antidote, somewhat on the homœopathic principle, that "like cures like." This they managed by boring a deep hole in the tree with an auger, into which a poor innocent shrew-mouse was thrust alive, with appropriate incantations. The entrance being then plugged up, of course the wretched mouse shortly died, and the tree thenceforward became a wonderful "Shrew-Ash," and, as such, was treated with the greatest veneration; for when any animal was afflicted by a shrew, as aforesaid, all they had to do was to touch the limb gently with a twig of such a tree, and straightway the creature so tormented was cured!

THE ASH.

The foliage of the Ash gives food to several fine insects of the moth tribe; the finest of which, the rare and magnificent Clifton-non-pareil, receives its Latin specific name (*Catocala Fraxini*) from the Ash. Among the rest, are the Privet hawk-moth, the Wood-leopard-moth, the Scarlet tiger-moth, the Red-arches moth, and the common Footman-moth. The brilliant Blister-fly, (*Cantharis vesicatoria*), also, is very fond of the leaves but is only very sparingly met with in this country; but on the Continent is so abundant as frequently to strip the trees of their leaves, rendering, moreover, their vicinity very disagreeable, and even dangerous, from the nauseous, pungent odour, and the floating particles which they give off—and which, when inhaled, produce very deleterious effects.

The inner bark of the Ash is frequently mined by a small beetle, in a manner similar to that of the Elm, which will be presently described.

The Ash may be readily recognised in spring by the singular blackness of its buds.

THE ELM.[1]—(*Ulmus campestris.*)

THIS stately tree, notwithstanding its thoroughly English character, is one of those whose claim to be ranked as indigenous has been disputed by botanists, who allege that it was introduced here either by the Romans or the Crusaders. Be this as it may, the Elm has become perfectly naturalized in this country, and enjoys a much better right to be called English than all the good families who "came in with the Conquest." No tree, in fact, identifies itself more completely with our most characteristic English scenery, especially in conjunction with human habitations, from which it is seldom seen far distant. In painting a scene of English country life, is it not the Elm that first suggests itself as the appropriate tree to shade the village green, and to give a good framework to the homestead?

LEAF AND SEED VESSELS OF COMMON ELM.

Ulmus Campestris. Nat. order, *Ulmaceæ;* Lin. syst. *Pentandria Digynia.* Gen. char.: Calyx, 4 or 5-cleft, inferior, persistent; corolla, none; capsule, membranous, compressed, nearly flat, with 1 seed.—Spec. char.: Leaves rhomboid, ovate, doubly serrated, rough above, downy beneath; flowers nearly sessile; fruit oblong, deeply cloven, naked.

THE ELM.

A finely grown Elm is among the handsomest of trees; lofty, yet graceful, it is an especial favourite with artists, who delight in its well-balanced contour, and the fine effects of light and shade offered by its rich foliage,—dark green in summer, and in autumn taking a bright yellow hue that harmonizes beautifully with the deeper autumnal tints of other trees, such as the beech and oak. The Elm frequently towers to a great height, sometimes exceeding 100 feet, but more frequently varying from seventy to ninety feet, with a trunk of four or five feet in diameter.

There are in the country many very old and large Elms, some with historical associations rivalling in antiquity those of the famous old oaks, as they do also in the vastness of their hollow trunks.

We recollect once visiting an enormous specimen at Crawley, near Horsham in Sussex. The girth of the trunk, measured near the ground, was sixty-one feet, and round the inside of the cavity (for it was hollow) was thirty-five feet. The floor is paved with bricks, and the entrance to the hollow is by a regular door, which is generally locked, and the key is kept by the lord of the manor; but, on particular occasions, the neighbours meet and banquet in the cavity, which will accommodate more than a dozen persons.

The timber of the Elm is well known as a valuable material for many purposes of country carpentry, such as cart-building, &c. and is especially employed in situations where its durability, under alternations of wet and dry, renders it most serviceable, as in water-mill wheels, conduit pipes, pumps, &c.; and in naval architecture it is the chief timber used for laying the keels of large ships, and for planking below the water-line.

Evelyn informs us that the leaves were formerly gathered in sacks in Hertfordshire as fodder for swine and cattle, adding, that "they will eat them before oats, and thrive exceedingly well upon them." Feeders of cattle, living where the Elm is plentiful, and other food scarce, might occasionally profit by this knowledge.

The Elm has many insect enemies, of which the most destructive, and at the same time one of the most diminutive, is the little bark-boring beetle without an English name, but scientifically called *Scolytus destructor*. We sometimes see a prostrate Elm trunk by the roadside, with the bark in an unhealthy-looking, semi-decayed state. If we break off a piece of this bark we shall probably find the inner surface scored with numerous channels, which emanate from each side of a central line, like the map of a number of rivers rising from a long mountain ridge. These grooves are the work of the little Scolytus, whose agency brought down the giant tree now at our feet.

Sometimes these channels, instead of being parallel, diverge irregularly from a common centre, as in the adjoining figure, which is a reduced copy of a piece of mined bark we found not long since. In either case, however, the process by which all this came about is much the same, and a curious piece of insect engineering it is.

BARK OF THE ELM MINED BY THE SCOLYTUS.

In the month of July, the female Scolytus (a small beetle about a quarter of an inch long) eats or bores her way through the bark till she comes to the soft wood within: here she turns her course at right angles, and excavates a gallery through the inner bark in an upward direction, and about two inches in length, depositing as she proceeds a line of eggs on each side of this gallery. This done, and the devoted mother having thus provided for the welfare of her offspring, her part in life is finished; she never emerges from the cell she has formed with so much labour, and we may see her dead body at the end farthest from where she entered,—but she leaves behind those who will amply fill her place. In about two months the eggs are hatched, and each tiny grub begins to feed upon the inner bark, eating away a passage nearly at right angles to the large channel it was hatched in, and, of course, enlarging the tunnel with its own growth, till at last it has come to maturity, and, staying its progress, it turns first to a chrysalis, then to a beetle, and, gnawing a hole outwards into the air, emerges to lay the foundation of another colony of miners; and so on, till the unfortunate tree, from the gradually extended injury to its vital inner bark, can no longer maintain the circulation of the sap, which goes on through this part, and so lapses into ill-health and decay. Whole avenues of Elms have thus perished in some places.

The comparatively gigantic Goat Moth is, in the caterpillar state, another dangerous and sometimes fatal enemy to the Elm,—not confining itself to the bark, but by boring long galleries, large enough to admit the finger, through the solid heart-wood, it seriously depreciates the value of the otherwise sound timber, destroying the integrity of its substance, even if its injuries do not lead to the complete decay and fall of the tree, as sometimes is the case.

There is an eccentric little leaping beetle [1] (called, from that habit, the Elm-flea) sometimes found in troops

[1] Haltica.

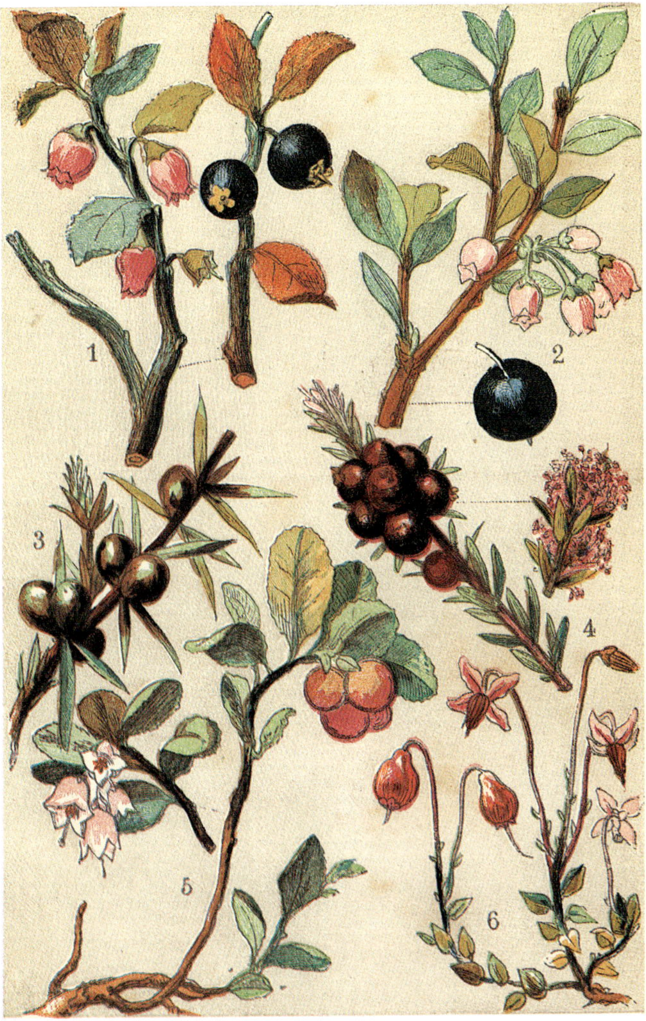
1
2
3
4
5
6

among the foliage, which it devours, without, however, doing much real damage to the tree. When magnified, it is found to be a splendid little creature, in its glittering armour of green and gold, with the thighs of its hinder legs surprisingly developed; and good use it makes of its extra muscles: a branch may be one moment covered with these pigmy hoppers; we make a movement to get out our magnifying glass,—and, *presto*, all have vanished; the branch is cleared in a twinkling.

The oddly-shaped Comma Butterfly, and the Elm Butterfly or Large Tortoise-shell, both feed on Elm-leaves; and the pretty Gold-tail Moth sometimes overruns the tree in the caterpillar state, half stripping it of its foliage.

THE WYCH ELM, OR SCOTCH ELM [1]

(*Ulmus montana*)

Is principally distinguished from the common English Elm by the character of its growth, which is less upright

[1] *Ulmus montana.* Nat. order, *Ulmaceæ.* Lin. syst.: *Pentandria Digynia.* Gen. char.: see page 34.—Spec. char.: Leaves obovate, pointed, doubly and coarsely serrated, nearly equal at the base, very rough above, downy beneath; flowers nearly sessile; fruit obovate, rather rhomboidal, slightly cloven, naked; branches drooping, smooth.

and more loose and spreading than that of the latter; its central trunk being less tall and continuous, and dividing at no great distance from the ground into long and rather drooping branches, forming a wide-spreading tree. As another mark of distinction, we may observe that the leaves are larger and broader shaped than those of the common Elm.

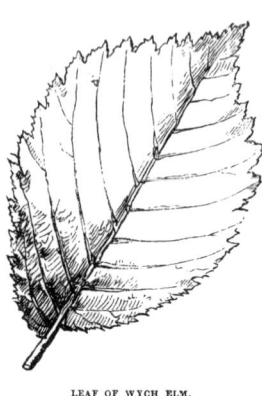

The Wych Elm is considered to be the real indigenous Elm of the country, and in Scotland is very frequent in a truly wild state, often forming the chief ornament of Scottish scenery. Some varieties have the branches quite pendulous, like the weeping willow, thus producing a most graceful effect. The trunk is often covered with huge, knotty excrescences, which add greatly to the picturesque character of the tree, and afford a highly-prized material for the cabinet-maker, being curiously marbled and veined. These are cut into very thin veneers, and applied to choice tables, cabinets, &c. The ordinary timber furnished by this tree is of excellent quality for many purposes, having more toughness longitudinally than

LEAF OF WYCH ELM.

the common Elm timber, so that it may sometimes be used as a substitute for the Ash.

This Elm frequently attains an immense size : there is one called the "Trysting Tree," near Roxburgh, in Teviotdale, whose girth, measured at four feet from the ground, is 30 feet. Another, felled some time since in Staffordshire, was 120 feet high, and the trunk 17 feet in diameter at the ground. It was probably from the mere coincidence between the names "wych" and "witch," that certain magical properties were attributed to the Wych Elm or Wych Hazel, as it is sometimes called. "In some of the midland counties, even to the present day, a little cavity is made in the churn, to receive a small portion of 'Wych-hazel,' without which the dairymaids imagine that they would not be able to get the butter to come."[1]

THE BIRCH.[2] (*Betula alba.*)

THOSE who are familiar with our mountain scenery will acknowledge how much of its romantic beauty is derived

[1] Loudon, Arboretum Britannicum.

[2] *Betula alba.* Nat. order, *Betulaceæ;* Lin. syst.: *Monœcia Tetrandria.* Gen. char. : Barren flower in a cylindrical catkin, its scales 3-flowered; perianth 0; stamens, 10-12; fertile flower,

from this most graceful, airy tree, so appropriately styled by Coleridge, "the Lady of the Woods." In every situation its presence is felt as adding a charm to the scene, whether waving on the brow of the cliff, with its light, transparent form seen quivering against the sky, or down on the shore of the broad loch, to which it forms a most harmonious foreground.

LEAF AND CATKIN OF BIRCH.

The Birch may be readily distinguished from other trees, at first sight, by the peculiar silvery whiteness of its bark, its slender form, and the comparative smallness of its leaves, which are shaped as in the accompanying figure. There are two principal varieties of this species, the erect, and the Weeping Birch,[1] the latter having by

scale of the catkin imperfectly 3-lobed, 3-flowered; perianth 0; styles 2; germens compressed, 2-celled, one abortive; nuts compressed, with a membranaceous margin, 1-seeded.—Spec. char.: Leaves ovato-deltoid, acute, doubly serrated glabrous.

[1] *Betulalaba, v. pendula.*

far the more characteristic elegance of the two, the lesser branches being more slender and drooping, and the leaves smaller, while the tree itself attains a much larger size than the other kind. The weeping variety is the one that prevails in the mountain districts of Scotland and Wales. It may be remarked that in ascending our loftiest mountains the Birch is the last tree that we miss on our upward path, for it continues with us to heights far above the level at which even the Scotch fir disappears.

In enumerating the uses of the Birch, we will discard from the list the imaginary virtues so long ascribed to it as an occasional *stimulant* and *alterative* in the scholastic training of British youth; its ancient reputation having lately fallen away "root and branch," so that it is no longer, as styled by Phillips, the

> " Afflictive birch,
> Cursed by unlettered idle youth, ..."

who, from the earliest ages, had good cause to regard it with terror. In old Gerarde's time this botanical remedy for juvenile frailty was in full vogue, as appears from his observations, that "schoolmasters and parents do terrifie their children with rods made of Birch." Now, however, gentler means are found to work the desired amelioration far more surely and satisfactorily to both *doctor* and *patient.*

In the colder regions of the Continent, the wood and bark of the Birch are more universally made use of than is the case in Britain. The young spray, besides its uses for making brooms, &c., affords a capital fuel for the iron furnaces. The large old wood is manufactured into furniture and agricultural implements. The outer bark, which is almost imperishable, serves a variety of purposes; houses are roofed with it instead of tiles; and in Lapland, where the Birch is almost the sole tree, its utility is immense; of it the natives make baskets, mats, cordage, waterproof boots and shoes, and by taking a broad sheet of it, and cutting a hole in the middle for the head, a respectable "mackintosh" is produced. Strips of the bark twisted together form excellent torches, the inflammability being due to the presence of a quantity of oil, which when distilled is employed in the preparation of Russia leather, and gives to it its peculiar odour. For many of these purposes it is also used in the Highlands of Scotland, but its chief appliances in this country are for making packing-crates, and hoops for herring-barrels; and also as fire-wood. Birch charcoal is much used in manufacturing gunpowder, and well prepared sticks of it form excellent crayons for drawing.

The naturalist finds in Birch-woods plenty of interesting subjects, some of which are peculiar to such localities. That pretty bird of the finch tribe called the Siskin,[1]

[1] Fringilla spinus.

may here be seen busy with the seeds, which are its favourite food. Then there is a large number of insects, including some of those most prized by the collector, that feed on the leaves, either partially or exclusively. The rare and magnificent Camberwell Beauty is one of the former division, and the very pretty, though not brilliant, Brown-hair-streak, another Butterfly, is only met with in the neighbourhood of Birch-trees. We shall mention a few only of the Moths found, in more or less abundance, in Birch-woods.—The Lime Hawk Moth, the Wood Leopard Moth, the Swallow Prominent Moth, Lunar Marbled-brown Moth, Kentish Glory Moth, Black-arches Moth, Red-arches Moth, Blossom-underwing Moth, Light-orange-underwing Moth, Peppered Moth, Oak Beauty Moth, &c.

On very old trees we have found occasionally a massive fungus as large as a child's head, called the Birch Boletus, which when cut asunder is found to be composed of a pure white substance of corky texture; and we have used this for various purposes instead of cork, such as carving small models, which have a beautiful appearance. It also makes an excellent material for lining entomological boxes as a substitute for cork. That most poisonous of the mushroom genus, the Fly Agaric (*Agaricus muscarius*), though not growing on the tree, yet, being generally found in Birch-woods, should be noticed here. It is a very handsome fungus, having a bright red upper surface studded with brown warts. Its effects when taken in small quantities are highly narcotic, producing intoxication and delirium, and, if the dose be large, terminating in death.

THE DWARF BIRCH.[1] (*Bétula nána.*)

IN the Highlands of Scotland, especially in wet, boggy places, this elegant little shrub is found, forming a lowly bush seldom more than two or three feet in height. Though rather looked on as a botanical curiosity in Britain, it is a plant of immense importance to the inhabitants of barren Lapland, furnishing them with their chief fuel and bedding, while the seeds nourish the Ptarmigan, which in its turn becomes a most valuable article of food to the natives.

On the Dwarf Birch grows the *Boletus fomentarius*, from which the *amadou* or *moxa* is prepared, and which is held

DWARF BIRCH.

---

[1] *Betula nána.* Gen. char.: see page 41.—Spec. char.: Leaves orbicular, crenate.

by the Laplanders to be an efficacious remedy in many painful diseases.

This species is often cultivated as an ornamental shrub in collections.

THE SCOTCH PINE OR FIR.[1] (*Pinus sylvéstris.*)

OF all the numerous species of Pine and Fir met with in the parks and plantations of this country, only one, the Scotch Pine, is really indigenous to Britain, and that only in the northern parts of Scotland, where it becomes one of the most striking objects in the grand scenery there displayed; and those only who have seen it in its natural situation can appreciate its wild and picturesque beauty, in perfect harmony with the sublime features that surround it. It seems indeed hardly the same tree, amidst the refinement and smoothness of a southern pleasure-ground. That eminent critic and admirer of trees, Sir T. D. Lauder, a

[1] *Pinus sylvéstris.* Nat. order, *Pinaceæ;* Lin. syst.: *Monœcia Monadelphia.* Gen. char.: Male anthers, 2-celled; female scales in a conical cone, bracteate at base, digynous; pericarps attached to the inside of scale, more or less winged, deciduous; stigmas bifid, or trifid, cotyledons, 4-8.—Spec. char.: Leaves in pairs, rigid; cones conico-ovate, acute, as long as the leaves generally in pairs.

native of Scotland, thus speaks in rapturous enthusiasm of his national tree :—" When its foot is amongst its own Highland heather, and when it stands freely on its native knoll of dry gravel, or thinly covered rock, over which its roots wander far in the wildest reticulation, while its tall, furrowed, often gracefully sweeping red and grey trunk, of enormous circumference, raises aloft its high umbrageous canopy, then would the greatest sceptic on this point (its picturesqueness) be compelled to prostrate his mind before it with a veneration which perhaps was never before excited by any other tree."

The name of "Fir," though in very general use, is erroneously applied to this tree, which really belongs to the division called Pines, broadly distinguished from the Firs by the different forms of the adult trees,—spreading and flat-headed in the former, and regularly conical or steeple-shaped in the latter, of which the Spruce Fir is a familiar example.

The Scotch Pine is considered to be the most valuable timber-tree of its tribe in Europe, producing the best of the material called deal, which is used to such an immense extent in civil and naval architecture ; the greater proportion of this kind of wood is, however, imported from the shores of the Baltic, especially Norway, as our own forests are quite inadequate to supply the enormous demand. Any detail of the manifold but well-known uses to which deal is put would be superfluous here.

We have often witnessed most beautiful pictorial effects in a group of Scotch Pines under the influence of the setting sun, whose warm rays, where they strike upon the red-barked stems and branches, light them up into bars of glowing crimson, magically contrasted with the deep gloom of the dark blue-green foliage. But however striking the character of the Pine, regarded under favourable circumstances, may be, it is pretty certain that an ordinary close-set Pine plantation, with the monotony of its endless ranges of straight poles, forms a scene far from cheerful or picturesque :—all verdure is banished from the ground beneath ; for the dense shade, together with the deleterious nature of the fallen leaves, is destructive to almost all other vegetation, and the Pines are left sole tenants of the soil.

The insects which attack and injure Pine and Fir trees in general, are far more numerous than would have been anticipated from the resinous nature of all the parts of these trees ; products of similar character being used to a large extent artificially for *driving away* insects ; but it seems that the constitutions of these little marauders are altered to fit them to the most unlikely food, so that some species depend for life upon what would be speedy death to others. The Giant Sirex[1] is one of these enemies that we have occasionally met with in the neighbourhood of Fir plantations,—a very formidable looking insect, in size and colour much like the venomous Hornet, but harmless, except to the timber it attacks. This it does by boring into the solid wood, when in the grub state, and feeding there till it changes to a *pupa*, and then emerges a perfect insect. On one occasion much astonishment and alarm was occasioned to a nurse and her juvenile charges by the unaccountable appearance of several great Sirexes coming suddenly out of the floor of the nursery, and buzzing terrifically about among the youthful company, who, unblest by science, knew not that their visitors were stingless. The explanation of this phenomenon is, that the deal flooring was newly laid down, and the boards must have contained the *pupæ* of the Sirex, which, coming to maturity in that situation, made their appearance as related.

If our readers should chance to find on a Fir-tree a large caterpillar, of bright green colour, with brown stripe down the back, terminating in a black, horny tail, let them carefully carry it home, taking a branch of Fir for it to feed on, and give it a box with some

[1] Syrex gigas.

loose earth at the bottom. If all goes well with it, it will change first into a brown chrysalis, then into a large and pretty moth—the Pine-hawk Moth [1]—which the captor may either keep as a rarity, or give to his entomological friend (if he has one), by whom it will be duly prized.

Multitudes of small insects of different orders frequent the Pine and Fir; some drilling the substance of the wood in all directions, and reducing the interior to dust; some nibbling the leaves, till the trees become bare; some channelling beneath the bark, like the *Scolytus* of the Elm; and others forming resinous galls at the end of the young shoots, in which the grubs reside.

The fungi found in Pine-woods are extremely numerous, and frequently distinguished by their great beauty of form or colour, many of them being peculiar to Pine-trees, either growing attached to some part of the tree, or among the dead leaves on the ground, and others even on the fallen cones. It will thus be seen that, notwithstanding the unpromising aspect of a Pine-wood, it is not by any means barren of interest to the naturalist.

[1] Sphinx Pinastri.

THE LARCH.[1] (*Lárix Europǽa.*)

This lofty, pyramidal tree may be distinguished from the spruce and other firs, and the pine—all which are of an evergreen nature—by losing its summer foliage, and remaining bare through the winter, retaining only the cones, which give a curious spotted appearance to the spray, when seen at a little distance, against the sky. A

CONES OF LARCH.

vast extent of land, especially in the northern parts of the kingdom, is now devoted to the cultivation of the Larch, as its excellent timber qualities, in some respects excelling those of the Scotch pine, are gaining due appreciation from landowners. As an ornamental tree, the Larch has little to recommend it, except that in spring a tree planted in a free space, so as to bear

[1] *Larix Europæa.* Nat. order, *Pinaceæ*; Lin. syst.: *Monœcia Monadelphia.* Gen. char. : Male anthers 2-celled; female, scales imbricated in a round cone, bracteate at base, digynous; pericarps attached to inside of scale, winged, deciduous; stigma hemispherical, cupped, glandular; cotyledons 5-9.—Spec. char. : Leaves fascicled, deciduous; cones ovate-oblong; edges of scales reflexed, lacerated, Bractes panduriform.

branches that sweep the ground, becomes an elegant object for the time, clothed in the delicate pea-green of its young leaves, and tasselled over with the beautiful pink flower-spikes. This beauty, however, soon gives place to the dinginess and poverty that characterise the tree during the rest of the year.

There are several other cone-bearing trees, more or less abundantly cultivated in plantations and mixed woods, but whose history we have not space to enter into. The principal of these are, the common or Norway Spruce Fir (*Abies excelsa*), a tall, evergreen, spire-shaped tree; the Silver Fir (*Picea pectinata*), similar in growth to the last, but somewhat less taper in form, and whose dark green leaves are marked on the under surface with two silvery white lines; the Pinaster (*Pinus Pinaster*), rather resembling the Scotch pine, but which may be known by its large clustered masses of foliage at the ends of the branches, giving the tree a peculiar tufted appearance.

THE FIELD MAPLE.[1] (*Acer campéstre.*)

THOUGH the Maple, from its valuable qualities as a hedge-bush, is generally confined to that position, we must class it among forest-trees, as it attains dimensions entitling it to that rank, when exempted from the pruning-hook and shears, and allowed to assume its natural form, which is that of a handsome and picturesque little tree, between twenty and thirty feet high when full grown. The leaves are of an elegant palmate shape, and give a peculiar crispness to the general aspect of the foliage; and in autumn they take varied tints of yellow and orange, which have a rich effect as forming part of the landscape.

LEAF, BLOSSOM, WINGED SEEDS, AND PORTION OF BRANCH OF MAPLE.

The bark is remarkably corky, and deeply furrowed,—this peculiarity being particularly noticeable in the young branches, and sufficing to distinguish the Maple from all other British trees.

[1] *Acer campestre.* Nat. order, *Acerineæ;* Lin. syst.: *Octandria Monogynia.* Gen. char.: Calyx 5-cleft, inferior; petals 5; germen 2-lobed; capsules 2, united at the base, each with a long winged membrane.—Spec. char.: Leaves mostly 5-lobed; lobes obtuse, notched, flowers in erect, corymbus-like racemes.

THE FIELD MAPLE.

This is one of an extensive genus, all the species of which abound in a saccharine juice; and from several of these sugar has been extracted on a large scale, especially from the Sugar-maples of America.

In this country, the wood is the sole valuable product of the Maple, it being close-grained, often very beautifully marked, and susceptible of a high polish—qualities which have caused it to be much used in cabinet-work and for turnery; but the kind most highly prized is that obtained from the knotty excrescences of the stem and roots, which are often most curiously veined and spotted, and, when highly polished, present a very rich appearance.

One of the hobbies in which the ancient luxurious Romans indulged (as the old-china mania was not then invented) was the acquisition, at enormous prices, of tables made from very rare and curious specimens of Maple-wood. Their wives also happened to have another costly taste, for dresses, jewellery, and the like vanities, which their lords, oblivious of their own rather expensive little fancies, considered were needless extravagances, and sometimes ventured to hint as much; when the ladies, roused by this injustice, would in their turn point to the sumptuous Maple-table, with an allusion to its ruinous price; and this was called *"turning the tables"* on their husbands;—hence the phrase used to this day for a similar kind of retort.

THE SYCAMORE.[1] (*Ácer Pséudo-plátanus.*)

WITH regard to the identity of this tree, a double confusion exists in the non-botanical mind. In the first place, as it is called in Scotland the Plane-tree, and it is very frequently confounded with the Oriental and Western Planes—trees of very different character to the Sycamore, but having leaves of rather similar shape.

Then, again, it is generally supposed to be the Sycamore mentioned in Scripture, as the tree on which Zacchæus climbed to see Christ as he passed on his way to Jerusalem; but the Sycamore of the Bible was really a kind of fig-tree, the *Ficus Sycomorus* of botanists; while the present tree is a species of Maple.

LEAF, FLOWERS, AND SEEDS OF SYCAMORE.

The Sycamore, when fully grown, forms a large, massive tree, with a contour often much resembling that of the oak; though the broadness of the individual

[1] *Acer Pseudo-platanus.* Nat. order, *Aceraceæ*: Lin. syst.: *Octandria Monogynia.* Gen. char.: see page 38.—Spec. char.: Leaves 5-lobed, unequally serrated; racemes pendulous.

THE SYCAMORE. 57

leaves gives a different and rather heavier character to the mass of its foliage, which, when fully developed, affords a more dense, impenetrable shade than almost any other tree; on which account we often see it planted close to the sunny side of the dairy, to the coolness of which its presence greatly contributes.

In spring, the half-expanded young leaves are extremely beautiful objects, showing, when held up to the light, the most delicate transparent tints of red, amber, and olive; but as the season advances, the leaves become opaque, and are usually disfigured by the attacks of insects, some of which perforate and render them ragged; while others (*Aphides*) exude from their bodies a clammy, sweet fluid, known as "honey-dew," which, covering the surface of the leaves, causes them to retain the dust that alights upon them, so that towards the end of summer the foliage presents a peculiarly dirty, unwholesome appearance, more especially observable in the neighbourhood of large towns, where smoke and its deposits are added to the dust of the road. The autumnal tints are nevertheless often very rich and harmonious, and are assumed earlier than those of many of its sylvan brethren. Cowper well describes the ever-varying hues of

> " The Sycamore, capricious in attire,
> Now green, now tawny, and ere autumn yet
> Has changed the woods, in scarlet honours bright."

The wood of the Sycamore is of a yellowish colour in mature trees; compact and firm in texture, without being very hard; and being easily worked, and susceptible of a high polish, it is in great request among turners, cabinet-makers, and musical instrument makers, with whom it is a favourite material for violins. As a fuel it is esteemed the best of all woods, both for the amount of heat it gives out, and the time it lasts while burning.

The sap, like that of all the maple tribe, holds in solution a considerable quantity of sugar, which has been separated from it, on a small scale, in Scotland, where the tree abounds; but the manufacture could not be profitably carried on as a commercial operation. The Scotch children amuse themselves by making incisions in the bark, and sucking the sweet sap that flows from the wound very freely; and from this liquor, by fermentation, a wine of tolerable quality may be made.

As an instance of the really magnificent dimensions an old Sycamore can attain to, we may mention one at Kew, a century old, which is seventy-four feet in height, and has a trunk five and a half feet thick; but in the north there are some specimens, the trunks of which much exceed the one at Kew.

THE LIME-TREE, OR LINDEN.[1]

(*Tilia Europæa*.)

THIS is better known as an inhabitant and ornament of our towns than as a wild woodland tree; and, in fact, the large-leaved kind, with which we are all familiar, is so seldom found growing in a state of nature, —that is, in localities where it was not probably planted by the agency of man,—that it is generally considered by botanists to have been a foreign variety introduced to this country from the Continent at a very distant period, and long since become naturalized here.

LEAF AND FLOWER OF LIME-TREE.

There is, however, a Lime-tree which we frequently meet with in woods far from human habitations, and, as it would seem, in a truly wild state, which

---

[1] *Tilia Europæa.* Nat. order, *Tiliaceæ ;* Lin. syst.: *Polyandria Monogynia.* Gen. char.: Calyx 5-parted, petals 5, capsule coriaceous, globose, 5-celled, 4-valved, opening at base, 1-seeded.— Spec. char.: Nectarines wanting, leaves smooth, except a woolly tuft at the origin of the veins beneath, cordate, acuminate and serrated, twice the length of the footstalks; cymes many-flowered, the capsule coriaceous and downy.

hardly differs from the common domesticated form, except in its smaller and less transparent leaves, and is known as the Small-leaved Lime-tree. In Essex and Sussex this kind is particularly abundant.

If the regularity of form which distinguishes the Lime prevents its ranking as one of our most picturesque trees, we must certainly regard it as one of the pleasantest and most cheerful, especially in early summer, when the eye is charmed by the fresh verdure of its foliage, the sense of smell delighted by the rich fragrance of its blossoms, while the ear is engaged by the music of the honey-bee and other insects, which in thousands flock to its honeyed stores.

Those who only know the Lime as an avenue-tree, —often cropped and stunted,—can form but little idea of the luxuriance of its growth, and the enormous dimensions it is capable of attaining when favoured by soil and situation. At Moor Park, in Hertfordshire, are some magnificent specimens, one of which is 100 feet high, with a head 122 feet in diameter, and a trunk 23 feet in circumference; but the most remarkable Lime-tree in this country is probably that at Knowle, in Kent, which, in extent of branchy canopy, and singularity of growth, rivals the famous Indian Banyan. The lower branches of this tree, after extending on every side to a great length, have drooped by their own weight till their extremities rested on the earth, in which they took root, and sent up a circle of young trees, which thus surrounded the parent stem. After a time, the outer branches of these latter, stretching out till they reached the ground, rooted there in their turn, and threw up a second circle of trees; so that at present this vast, vegetable curiosity, all emanating from a single stem, covers about a quarter of an acre of ground with its branches.

Besides the ornamental qualities possessed by the Lime, it is not without its direct service to man. The wood, which is yellowish-white in colour, soft, smooth-grained, and light, is put to a variety of useful purposes by cabinet-makers, turners, toy-makers, and carvers. The sounding-boards of pianofortes are made of it, as it does not warp under changes of atmosphere,—a quality which likewise recommends it for carriage-paneling. But the most elegant application of this wood is for fine carving, in the practice of which art it is justly preferred to every other wood :—

> "Smooth Linden best obeys
> The carver's chisel; best his curious work
> Displays in nicest touches."

The exquisite productions of Grinling Gibbons, executed in this material some two hundred years ago, may be seen in St. Paul's Cathedral, at Windsor Castle, Chatsworth, and other places, still looking sharp, delicate, and beautiful as when they came from the artist's chisel.

That well-known commodity called "bast-matting," and so useful to gardeners for protecting their plants, and to upholsterers for packing large goods, is a product of the Lime-tree, being prepared from the inner bark by macerating it in water till it separates into thin layers, strips of which are afterwards woven together into the form in which we see it.

The honey which bees obtain from Lime-blossoms is esteemed beyond every other kind, being very delicious and high-flavoured; but of course it can only be had pure in districts covered with forests of this tree, as in the case at Kauno, in Lithuania, where the honey is gathered immediately after the Lime has finished blossoming, and its sale,—at three or four times the price of common honey,—is the chief dependence of the inhabitants.

In some places, an infusion, or tea, made of Lime-blossoms, is held in great repute as a remedy for coughs, hoarseness, &c. ; and, from what we know of its qualities, it may probably be very efficacious in mild cases : at least the potion will be harmless and not unpleasant. Gilbert White informs us that he made some **Lime-blossom tea**, "and found it a very soft, well-flavoured, pleasant saccharine julep, in taste much resembling the juice of liquorice."

Amongst the numerous caterpillars who make the foliage of the Lime their food, we can only enumerate a few of the principal:—the Lime-hawk Moth (a beautiful insect in its perfect state, with wings of very singular shape, and exquisitely shaded with tints of olive-green, grey, and brown), the Buff-tip, Lobster Moth, Glory of Kent, Dagger Moth, Orange Moth, Brindled Beauty, Merveil-du-jour, Canary-shouldered Thorn Moth, &c.

THE WALNUT.[1]—(*Júglans régia.*)

THE Walnut, it may be said, belongs more properly to the orchard department than to that of forest-trees; but the country rambler so frequently meets with it in a half-wild looking state, by the roadside or in the park, grouping most picturesquely with other trees and with rustic architecture, and its importance as a timber and fruit-tree is so great, that we must introduce it as a member of our Sylva, along with the Horse-chestnut

[1] *Juglans regia.* Nat. order, *Juglandaceæ;* Lin. syst. *Monœcia Polyandria.* Gen. char.: Male, an imbricated catkin; calyx, a scale; corolla, 6-parted; filaments, 4-18. Female, calyx, 4-cleft; superior corolla, 4-cleft; styles 2; drupe coriaceous, with a furrowed nut.—Spec. char.: Leaflets about nine, oval, smooth, subserrated, nearly equal; fruit globose.

and Spanish chestnut, which have similar claims to that title.

The most valuable product of the Walnut is the fruit,[1] which is so well known, together with the

LEAF AND FRUIT OF WALNUT.

uses to which it is put, both in its green and mature state, that it would be superfluous to describe it here : we may, however, just mention, that there is one variety not often seen, which produces nuts nearly as large as a turkey's egg, but, notwithstanding their magnificent appearance, these are of inferior quality to some of the smaller sorts.

[1] The Walnut must have been highly esteemed by the ancients, and considered by them as food fit for the gods, as its Latin name *Juglans* is well known to be contracted from the words *Jovis, glans, i.e.* the acorn of Jove.

The timber of the Walnut, also, is in high estimation for cabinet-work, although not now used to the same extent as formerly, before the introduction of mahogany and other beautiful foreign woods; but some of the fine old Walnut furniture will bear comparison on all points with the most elegant productions of the present day.

Another most important use of Walnut-wood is for the manufacture of gun-stocks, for which its great strength and lightness especially qualify it.[1] The number of Walnut-trees grown in this country has, however, very greatly diminished of late years, as it has been found that a supply equal to the demands of the country can easily be obtained from the coasts of the Black Sea, and from America.[2]

The Walnut sometimes attains to grand dimensions, —one at Cothelstone, in Devonshire, being sixty-four feet high, with a trunk six and a half feet in diameter; and there are many very fine specimens in the neighbourhood of London.

The bark of this tree is grey and smooth on the upper branches, deeply furrowed on the trunk, and the

[1] About the year 1806, some twelve thousand Walnut-trees were annually required in France for the manufacture of muskets.

[2] The timber imported from America is that of the American walnut (*Juglans nigra*), a distinct species, but possessing similar qualities.

leaves are light and elegant both in form and colour. These have the defect of dropping off with the first frosts; but the tree, even in its denuded state, maintains its picturesque character, owing to the fine form and play of its bold branches.

From the austere nature of the juices in the leaves and other parts of the Walnut, it is attacked by very few insects. Among the moths, two species are recorded by Mr. Selby,—that known as the Peppered Moth, and another small *Geometra*.

THE EATABLE OR SPANISH CHESTNUT.[1]

(*Castánea vésca.*)

HAD we before us at once an Oak and a Chestnut, each in their maturity and perfection—and were it pos-

[1] *Castanea vesca.* Nat. order, *Corylaceæ*: Lin. syst.: *Monœcia Polyandria.* Gen. char.: Barren flower in a very long cylindrical catkin; perianth, single, of 1-leaf, 6-cleft; stamen, 5-20. Fertile, flower 3, within a 4-lobed, thickly muricated involucrum; perianth, single, urceolate, 5-6 lobed, having the rudiments of 12 stamens; germen incorporated with the perianth, 6-celled, with the cells 2-seeded, 5 of them mostly abortive; styles 6; nut 1-2, seeded, invested with the enlarged involucre.—Spec. char.: Leaves oblong, lanceolate, acuminate, mucronate, serrate, glabrous on each side.

sible to divest our minds of the heart-stirring associations belonging to the former—making outward beauty and magnificence the sole points of rivalry, we should long hesitate in giving the palm of superiority to either, as they both possess to an eminent degree picturesque qualities of their own, that commend them to our fullest admiration.

In colossal grandeur the Chestnut is scarcely inferior to the oak, excelling the latter in the rich character of its foliage, composed of large handsome leaves of glossy green; and often, also, in the fine forms presented by the trunk, the bark of which in old trees is full of deep rugged clefts. The ramification, too, when bared by winter of its verdure, is seen to have all the boldness and easy flow so remarkable in that of the oak.

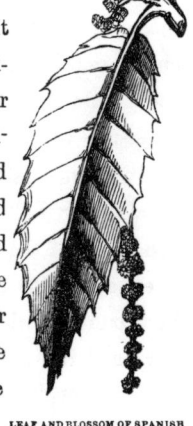

LEAF AND BLOSSOM OF SPANISH CHESTNUT.

When, however, we quit the merely artistic view we have been taking, and consider the absolute value of the oak commercially and historically, there is no question of its claim to sovereignty, since the Chestnut as a timber-tree is comparatively worthless. The age which gives heartiness and strength to the oak, brings shakiness and decay to the chestnut. Among the most remarkable chestnuts of this country is that at Tortworth, in Gloucestershire, which in King Stephen's days was so large as to be called the Great Chestnut of Tortworth. When last measured it was 52 feet in girth. There are also some very fine old trees to be seen in Kensington Gardens and Greenwich Park.

One of the best purposes, it is said, to which Chestnut wood can be applied is for making wine-casks, as it is less apt to taint the wine than any other wood, and thoroughly prevents evaporation. This use of Chestnut wood is referred to by Rapin, in his poem, "The Garden:"—

"With close-grained chestnut, wood of sov'reign use,
For casking up the grape's most potent juice."

The fruit of the Chestnut seems to be held in much less esteem by the English than by the natives of most other countries where it abounds. In some parts of France and Italy, chestnuts are used in great measure as substitutes for potatoes, and even bread, forming often a chief article of food for the poorer inhabitants. There are some scientific recipes for preparing them with milk, eggs, and various other additions; and in this state they form very popular dishes, sometimes rising to the rank of luxuries. The odour of the flowers is very powerful and peculiar, rendering the neighbourhood of the tree absolutely offensive to some people during the blossoming season.

But few insects frequent the Chestnut, and its foliage is almost entirely exempt from their attacks; but a kind of weevil[1] is often very injurious to the nuts, piercing them when very young and tender, and depositing its eggs in their substance. The fruit thus attacked never attains to maturity, dropping off when half-grown, and its interior of course becomes the prey of the inclosed grubs of the weevil.

THE HORSE CHESTNUT.[2]

(*Æsculus Hippocástanum.*)

Though both this tree and the last bear the name of Chestnut, no two trees can be much more botanically distinct than the Sweet Chestnut and the Horse Chestnut, which are very widely separated both in the Linnæan and natural systems of classification; yet we have heard them sometimes spoken of as being merely different species of the same genus, one adapted for the

[1] Pyrale Pflugione.

[2] *Æsculus Hippocastanum.* Nat. order, *Æsculaceæ;* Lin. syst.: *Heptandria Monogynia.* Gen. char.: Calyx 1-leaved, inflated; corolla 4-5 petaled, unequal, pubescent, inserted in the calyx; capsule 3-celled; seeds large, chestnut-like.—Spec. char.: Leaves digitate, 7; petals 5, spreading.

70   OUR WOODLANDS.

food of horses, the other for that of men ; an instance of the kind of error so frequently occurring from neglect of the scientific nomenclature, really indispensable in properly defining natural-history subjects. The chief point of resemblance between the two Chestnuts lies in the

LEAF OF HORSE CHESTNUT.

fact that they both produce nuts of similar aspect, although these differ very greatly in quality.

Nature can show few objects of greater magnificence than a princely Horse Chestnut-tree in early summer, when robed, as it is so aptly described by Sir T. D. Lauder, "in all the richness of its heavy velvet drapery, embroidered over with millions of silver flowers." Both the leaves and flowers are exceedingly beautiful when examined singly and closely, besides the striking effect they produce when massed together on the tree. The delicate white blossoms, tinted with yellow and rosy-red, and arranged in a hyacinth-like form, would grace a choice bouquet, and the symmetrical elegance of the ample leaves is unrivalled among native trees.

The anatomy of a bud of the Horse Chestnut, taken in the very early spring, affords one of the best instances of that wonderful arrangement of nature by which a minute bud is made to contain a large number of incipient flowers or leaves, which, notwithstanding their microscopic smallness, are perfect miniatures of the coming leaves and blossoms. To exemplify this, we quote the following experiment from the Magazine of Natural History, and any of our readers who have access to a Horse Chestnut-tree may verify it for themselves. "A celebrated German naturalist detached from this tree in the winter season a flower-bud not larger than a pea, and first took off the external covering, which he found consisted of seventeen scales. Having removed these scales, and the down which formed the internal covering of the bud, he discovered four branch leaves surrounding a spike of flowers, the latter of which were so distinctly visible, that, with the aid of a microscope, he not only counted sixty-eight flowers, but could discern the pollen of the stamens, and perceive that some was opaque, and some transparent."

The Horse Chestnut is planted in this country almost

solely for its highly ornamental qualities as a tree, as neither the fruit nor timber is of much value; the nuts being bitter and uneatable by man, and the wood soft, weak, and only applicable to a few purposes where neither strength nor durability are required.

This tree is said to have been brought to England from the mountains of Thibet, some time about the middle of the sixteenth century.

THE WILD PEAR TREE.[1]—*Pyrus commúnis.*

IN our spring rambles through the woods we occasionally come upon a tall, handsome tree, bearing a profusion of white flowers among its young green leaves: this is the Wild Pear-tree, from which were derived, by cultivation, all those choice varieties that grace the dessert-table; a wonderful change to be accomplished merely by the gardener's art, when we compare the austere little wilding fruit with the goodly *Jargonelles*, or *Beurrées*, so ample in size and luscious in flavour.

We must not, however, descant on the uses and per-

[1] *Pyrus communis.* Nat. order, *Pomaceæ;* Lin. syst.: *Icosandria di-pentagynia.* Gen. char.: Calyx with 5 segments; petals 5; styles 2-5; fruit fleshy, with 5 distinct, cartilaginous, 2-seeded cells.—Spec. char.: Leaves simple, ovate, serrated; flower stalks corymbose; fruit turbinate.

fections of the cultivated pear, as our chief concern in this volume is with those objects met with in a wild state. As the fruit of the Wild Pear is small and hardly eatable, the wood is the only part of the tree of any real value; this is very compact and fine-grained, and has been used for fine carvings, and once was the chief material from which wood engravings were executed. The curious old cuts in Gerarde's Herball were probably on this wood; but for this purpose it is greatly inferior to box, now the only wood used for engraving subjects wherein delicacy of execution is required. Pear-wood, when dyed black, so closely imitates ebony, that it can with difficulty be distinguished from it, and in this state it is used for picture-frames, and innumerable purposes of fancy or utility.

THE WILD APPLE OR CRAB-TREE.[1]

(*Pyrus Málus.*)

FAR more frequent in our woods and thickets than the pear, is the Wild Apple, which, though a low tree, stumpy and graceless in form, puts forth every season such an array of white and rosy blossoms, that when

[1] *Pyrus Malus.* Gen. char.: see page 72.—Spec. char.: Leaves ovate, rugose, serrated; flowers in a simple sessile umbel; styles united below; fruit globose.

seen in May, with these in their perfection, it yields to few plants in beauty, and forms one of the greatest spring ornaments to the woods it inhabits.

The Wild Apple bloom, too, is not only beautiful in mass, but a sprig, when gathered and examined in detail, is, perhaps, still more lovely, the curled and crumpled petals being varied with every delicate shade, from satiny white to deep rose red. The ripe fruit, also, has external beauties of its own, but there let our commendation rest, for the sourness and austerity of its taste are proverbial, "*crab*biness" being, as we know, synonymous with all that is the reverse of sweet and pleasant.[1] Yet this little sour fruit is the origin of most of our esteemed orchard and garden apples, the vast difference between them being the result of assiduous cultivation.

A large number of insects of various orders inhabit and feed on both the wild and cultivated apple tree, the most important of which, not indeed for its use or beauty, but on account of the injury it works, is that called the Woolly Aphis,[2] a little creature that produces that white downy matter sometimes seen covering the stems and branches of the tree, which when thus infected become cankered, and ere long perish. The mischief, however, is not caused by this white substance itself, which is merely a secretion, thrown out by the

[1] Verjuice is the expressed juice of the Crab.
[2] Eriosoma Mali.

THE WILD APPLE OR CRAB TREE. 75

insect as a protection to it while engaged in feeding on the life juices of the tree; for if a tuft of this "blight," as it is called, is closely examined, tiny soft insects will be found, crouching close to the bark, and resembling the Aphides so common in the rose and other plants. Various remedies have been tried, to destroy this pest, but all of them involve much labour, and in large orchards its extermination is hopeless.

Every one has experienced the annoyance of finding a tempting apple all worm-eaten within, and the track of the spoiler defiled with dust and rottenness; but few have marked the curious economy of the little animal that has forestalled us in the enjoyment of our fruit. About Midsummer, a beautiful little moth, studded with silver specks, may be seen visiting the newly-set apples, and depositing in the eye of each a single egg; this, shortly hatching, produces a tiny grub, that, forthwith, sets to work, and eats his way deep into the substance of the young apple, but studiously keeping clear of the vital core (any injury to which would cause the premature fall of his home) until the apple and himself are together approaching maturity, when he at last makes for the core, and changing his diet, feeds away the last days of his grubhood upon the nutty pips; these being destroyed, the apple seems as if struck to the heart, and speedily drops to the ground. This is just what our little friend desired, tired even of fragrant pips, he wanted a thorough change in life—to see the world, in fact—and the apple's fall is the signal for him to move. A passage which he had long ago tunnelled through to the air, to afford him a supply of that element, now serves him as a means of exit; and emerging therefrom, he seeks the nearest tree trunk, crawls up it, and, finding a snug crevice, ensconces himself therein, fitting up the chosen spot for winter-quarters, by the addition of a white silk lining and curtain. Here he snoozes away the winter long as a chrysalis, being one of those gentry that don't care much for life, except in "the season," and June being "the season" with his circle, he then appears in society, a dandy of the first water, profuse with his silver studs, and carrying a name that many a foreign Count would be glad of; "*Carpocapsa pomanella,*" is his card, and if he isn't conceited, he might well be—but we forget—he is only the grub that spoilt the apple for us, after all.

The pretty little Ermine Moth [1] commits great ravages on the leaves of the Apple tribe; but though its biography is most interesting, we must omit it here, lest it be said we are forgetting the trees for the insects that live on them.

From our own experience, the Mistletoe is found parasitic upon the Crab far more frequently than upon any other tree.

[1] Tinea padella.

THE WILD SERVICE TREE.[1]

Pyrus torminális. (Plate C, fig. 2.)

In situations where the Wild Crab flourishes, and especially in the southern parts of the kingdom, we may often meet with the Service Tree. It has been found in many places in the vicinity of London, among others at Caen Wood, near Hampstead; near Chingford in Epping Forest; and we have seen it growing luxuriantly on the chalk hills about Caterham, in Surrey. It makes an ornamental tree, both from the richness of its broad and curiously-shaped leaves, added to the large clusters of white flowers which appear in May, and from the profuse bunches of brown fruit, garnishing every branch in Autumn. The leaves are, when full-sized, nearly four inches long, and three inches broad in the middle (our figure was drawn from a small specimen, to avoid crowding the plate); the fruit is of a greenish brown when ripe, and of an acid, rough flavour; which, however, becomes very agreeable when the fruit is in a state of incipient decay, and mellowed by frost. In this condition we have sometimes seen it brought to market by country people, who string several hundreds of the berries

[1] *Pyrus Torminalis.* Gen. char.: see page 72.—Spec. char.: Leaves ovate or cordate, serrated, 7-lobed; the lower lobes divaricating; flower-stalks cymo-corymbose, branched.

together round a stick, so as to form a large cylindrical cluster, a yard long or more.

This tree does not generally grow to a large size, but has been known to attain the height of fifty-four feet, with a trunk three and a half feet thick.

The wood is very hard and close-grained, and valuable for making various small articles of turnery, &c.; but it is not sufficiently abundant to have much importance in this respect.

THE WHITE BEAM TREE.[1]

Pyrus Aria. (Plate C, fig. 1.)

WHAT a striking ornament to the rocky limestone districts in which it abounds, is the White Beam Tree, especially in the Autumn, with its liberal clusters of rich scarlet berries, contrasting powerfully with the snowy under-sides of the leaves, displayed by every breath of wind! This tree is not uncommon in the chalk-hills of Kent and Surrey, but we consider that, like the mountain ash, it appears to infinitely greater advantage in the situations first mentioned, where the

[1] *Pyrus Aria.* Gen. char.: see page 72.—Spec. char.: Leaves ovate, cut, serrated; hoary beneath; flowers in a dense flat corymbus; fruit globose.

THE WHITE BEAM TREE.

grey of the limestone-rock gives full value to the bright-coloured fruit and foliage, relieved upon it.

The fruit is full of a mealy, acid pulp, becoming sweeter when kept till over-ripe, and then not disagreeable to eat. A kind of beer may be obtained by fermenting the berries, and by distillation they afford a strong spirit. Small birds and animals, especially the hedge-hog, are exceedingly fond of the fruit, and devour it greedily.

The wood, though usually of small size, is not without its value, being extremely hard and fine-grained, of a yellowish tint, and taking a high polish. Its chief use is for making cogs for wheels used in machinery, for which purpose it is universally employed where iron has not superseded wood in millwork. Musical instruments are also made of it, as well as handles to cutlery, walking-sticks, wooden spoons, and various small turnery articles, in some of which it forms a good substitute for boxwood. The White Beam Tree has had several synonymes bestowed on it, among which are, Red Chess-Apple, Cumberland Hawthorn, White Wild Pear, and Sea Ouler.

THE MOUNTAIN ASH, OR ROAN TREE.[1]

Pyrus Aucupária.   (Plate C, fig. 3.)

BETWEEN the trim suburban garden, and the grim Highland steep, there is, doubtless, a vast constitutional difference; so that, in general, an object harmonizing with the one, would seem to be totally discordant with the other; yet the Mountain Ash oversteps the difficulty, and with easy grace accommodates itself to either situation. But ornamental as it is to the villa, we fancy there are few who would not prefer it in its native locality, as a wild mountaineer, in which character it claims our enthusiastic admiration. How lovely is its Spring foliage, of airiest lightness, and freshest verdure, every branch decked with large tufts of fragrant and conspicuous cream-white flowers. But the season of its greatest and characteristic beauty is when the flowers have given way to the glowing orange fruit, with which Autumn loads every bough. Then, peculiarly, is it the Mountain Ash beloved by poet and painter, and associated in our own mind with scenery, the grandest and the fairest we have witnessed.

From very early times, the Roan Tree enjoyed a

[1] *Pyrus Aucuparia.* Gen. char.: see page 72.—Spec. char.: Leaves pinnated; leaflets uniform, smooth, serrated; flowers corymbose; fruit globose.

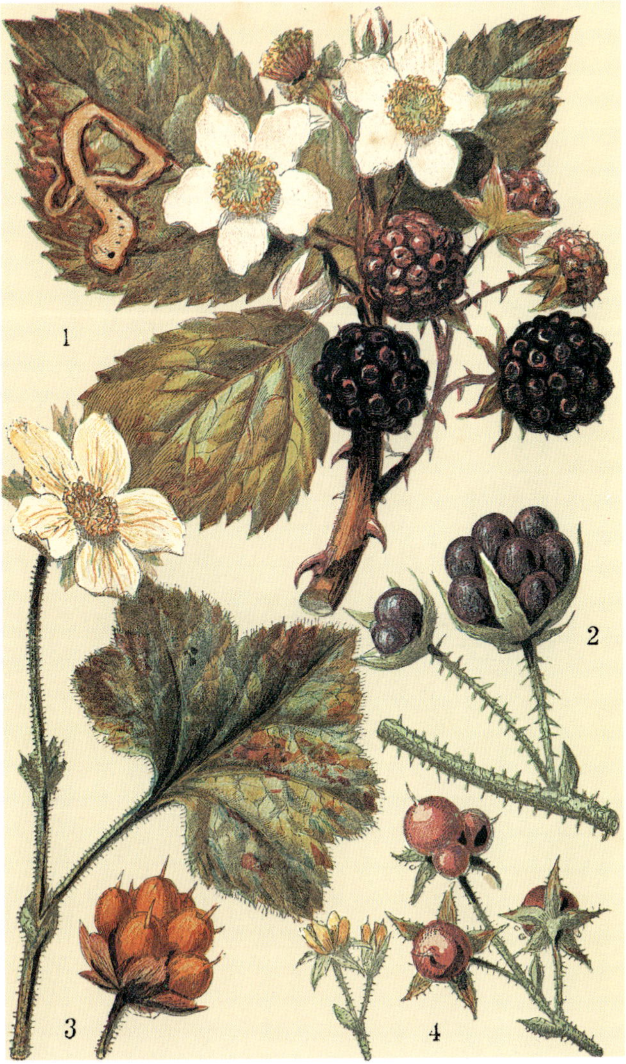
1
2
3
4

THE MOUNTAIN ASH, OR ROAN TREE. 81

wide reputation, not so much for its external beauty, as for the inherent magical powers attributed to it, by virtue of which its presence was considered to prove a sovereign charm against the evil machinations of witchcraft; and the superstition still lingers in sequestered districts, especially in the Highlands of Scotland and in Wales, "where it is often hung up over doorways, and in stables and cow-houses, to neutralize the wicked spells of witches and warlocks." A stump of the Roan Tree has been frequently found in the old buryingplaces and stone circles of the Druids, probably a relic of the tree planted by them for its sacred shade.

Turning from the picturesque or romantic, to the utilitarian view of this tree, we find that both wood and fruit serve a variety of good purposes. The wood, when it can be obtained of sufficiently large size, is applied to the same uses as that of the White Beam-tree, which it very nearly resembles in quality; and it used to be esteemed next to Yew for bows. The beautiful fruit is a very favourite food of birds, especially of the thrush tribe, who never cease their attentions to the trees while a berry remains; nor is it without its direct utility to man. Evelyn tells us that "ale and beer brewed with these berries being ripe is an incomparable drink, familiar in Wales." These berries are even eaten raw as a fruit, but we cannot recommend them, except as curiosities, for they are harsh and austere, with a nauseous under-taste, so that, with most persons, one will suffice for a dose.

Bird-catchers, taking advantage of the fondness of the feathered tribes for these berries, make them the chief bait to the horse-hair nooses, which they lay in the woods, to catch fieldfares, redwings, and other birds. In reference to this, the Mountain Ash is often called the Fowler's Service-tree; and the following synonymes are among those applied to it in various districts,— Quicken Tree, Quick Beam, Mountain Service, Rowan Tree, Witchen Tree, and Wiggen Tree. The term "witchen," of which "wiggen" is only a corruption, relates to the supposed anti-*witch*craft properties of the tree.

THE MEDLAR.—(*Méspilus germánica.*)

THE Medlar is not unfrequently found in a wild state in woods and coppices in Sussex, Kent, and Surrey; in the latter county, Redhill, Reigate, and between Rei-

[1] *Mespilus germanica.* Nat. order, *Pomaceæ:* Lin. syst.: *Icosandria di-pentagynia.* Gen. char.: Calyx 5-parted, with leafy divisions; disk large, honey bearing; styles smooth; apple turbinate, open, 5-celled, with a bony rectamen.—Spec. char.: Leaves lanceolate, entire or sub-serrate, a little downy; flowers solitary, nearly sessile, terminal; styles (mostly) 5.

gate and Nutfield, have been given as more definite localities where it may be met with. It forms a tree of the size and shape of an ordinary apple-tree, and may be readily known by its fantastically twisted branches, its fine large leaves, and solitary white flowers, about an inch broad, which appear in May and June; but in the Autumn, the tree is sufficiently marked by the peculiar and well-known fruit, which hardly differs in its

FLOWER AND LEAF OF MEDLAR.

wild and cultivated states—some of the garden varieties being merely increased in size. The Medlar is one of those fruits which the French style "*fruits de fantaisie,*" in contradistinction to those of utility; and, in fact, the Medlar-tree must be considered, altogether rather as an ornamental object than a profitable one, being a very desirable addition to the shrubbery for the sake of its fine foliage and blossoms.

THE ALDER.[1]—(*Álnus glutinósa.*)

THOUGH the Alder, considered individually, is by no means one of our handsomest trees, it is so intimately associated with our recollections of picturesque river-scenery,—either of that tranquil sylvan character so general in the lowland vales, or of the wilder nature met with in the deep glens and ravines of the mountain country,—that we always look upon this tree with interest and pleasure. The Alder also loves to fringe the margins of our lakes and pools, and in all these situations becomes a characteristic and

LEAF AND CATKINS OF ALDER.

---

[1] *Alnus glutinosa.* Nat. order, *Betulaceæ;* Lin. syst.: *Monœcia Tetrandria.* Gen. char.: Flowers collected into imbricated catkins (amenta); barren flower; catkins elongated, cylindrical; scales 3-lobed, 3-flowered; calyx 4-parted. Fertile flower, catkins ovate, scales obscurely 3-cleft, 2-flowered; calyx none; styles 2; nuts compressed.—Spec. char.: Leaves roundish, somewhat wedge-shaped, glutinous, the margin lobed and serrated; downy at the axils of the veins beneath.

ornamental adjunct,[1]—although, we think, that in too large masses the intensely-deep green of its foliage, is apt to produce a heavy and gloomy effect.

This tree has a considerable commercial value, and it is sometimes a very profitable one to the planter, from the fact that it will grow in situations too watery for even the willow and poplar, being, indeed, the most thoroughly aquatic of our native trees. Under the most favourable conditions, the Alder grows to a height of 60 or 70 feet, with a trunk of proportionate thickness; but, from 30 to 50 feet is its more usual range of height. We never observe this tree on a dry chalky soil.

The wood is white while the tree is standing; but, on being cut, it assumes a pale flesh-coloured tint, which it permanently retains. It is of a soft, even texture, and is a favourite material for many purposes of the turner and the wood-carver; various household vessels are made of it; also clogs and wooden soles for shoes. In France great numbers of the peculiar wooden shoes, called "*sabots*," are made of Alder. When dyed black, either artificially, or by long submersion in peat-bogs, it is very commonly substituted for ebony, although it is inferior in hardness and lustre to that wood.

Alder-wood, if kept constantly under water, is almost

[1] Those who have wandered along the banks of the Mole in Surrey, will acknowledge that much of its peculiar charm is really owing to the presence of the Alder, which there grows in great perfection.

imperishable, and therefore is most valuable for making piles, &c. It is said that on Alder-piles the beautiful arch of the famous Rialto of Venice is supported.

In the neighbourhood of gunpowder factories we often see large plantations of this tree, as the wood furnishes one of the best kinds of charcoal used in making that explosive compound.

THE WILLOW.[1]

THE study and classification of this extensive genus involves difficulties which have puzzled, not only the tyro in botany, but even the accomplished professor of the science, who finds himself at a loss when trying only to determine the number of really distinct species he may have before him,—the produce, it may be, of a single botanical excursion. Out of the group he will select several forms which correspond with what he has been accustomed to recognise as so many decided species;

[1] *Salix.* Nat. order, *Salicaceæ;* Lin. syst.: *Diœcia Diandria.* Gen. char.: Barren flower—scales of the catkin single-flowered, imbricated, with a nectariferous gland at its base; perianth 0; stamens 75. Fertile flower—scales of the catkin single flowered; perianth 0; stigmas 2, often cleft; capsule 1-celled, 2-valved, many-seeded seeds comose.

THE WILLOW. 87

but, this done, he will find remaining a number of doubtful forms intermediate between his so-called species, and which he can ascribe to neither. The leaves perhaps approach to those of one species, while the catkins or flowers are those of another; and the complication is increased by the fact that the Willows belong to that section of trees that have the male and female flowers on separate plants; so that at last the perplexed botanist, finding that the Willows refuse to be woven into his system, gives up the point, and resigns the subject to the laborious, plodding German mind, to which the very intricacy of the study serves as a charm and a stimulus.

With minute technicalities, and the quibbles of classification, however, we have no concern here; and it will be found that, practically, the differences that characterize the Willows may be resolved into a very few broad divisions. Thus, an ordinary observer of country objects, if asked to enumerate the various kinds of Willow that had come under his notice, would find, probably, that he had no clearly defined recollection of more than, at most, half-a-dozen different sorts. Prominent among these would be the Weeping-Willow, drooping its delicate pensile branches over the lake or lawn (but this species, by-the-bye, is not an indigenous native of Britain); then there would be the White Willow, either with a pollard top, or rising into a large timber-tree; next might be mentioned the humble osier, growing in beds by the river-side, and furnishing material for basket-work; the grey-foliaged sort that produces, in very early spring, those yellow blossoms so well known as "Palms," would make a fourth variety; and beyond these he would have a somewhat vague impression of having seen a Willow with very yellow twigs (the Golden Willow), and another, with small, dark, rounded leaves, which would conclude his list of British Willows. Having arrived at this result, he would probably be a little astonished to learn that some botanists make out more than seventy species indigenous to Britain, distinguished principally by their minute details, but all connected by similar habits and general features.

We shall now give, separately, brief descriptions of the species which may be regarded as representatives of the more obvious groups into which the Willows are divided by broad characteristics: beginning with

THE COMMON WHITE WILLOW.[1]—(*Sálix álba.*)

THIS is the Willow more extensively planted as a timber-tree than any other species; and, when not dis-

---

[1] *Salix alba.* Gen. char.: see page 86.—Spec. char.: Leaves elliptic, lanceolate, acute, serrated, permanently silky on both sides, the lowest serratures glandular; stamens hairy; stigmas deeply cloven.

THE COMMON WHITE WILLOW.

figured by the system of pollarding prevalent in many districts, is at the same time the finest and most picturesque of its tribe; growing to a very large size, and forming an elegant and imposing tree, its feathery foliage takes a silvery tint whenever a ruffling breeze exposes the white under-surface of the leaves; and when seen in conjunction with trees of deeper tint, on the margin of a river or lake, it constitutes a most agreeable and interesting feature in the landscape.

Even the stunted pollard, too, is not without its pictorial value, being often introduced by painters to give character to aquatic scenery, and to mark the course of a river in the mid-distance.

LEAF AND MALE FLOWERS OF WHITE WILLOW.

Dr. Johnson's Willow at Lichfield, one of the largest on record, was of a species similar in size and character to the present, and known as the Bedford Willow (*Salix Russelliana*).

The timber of both these kinds is of an elastic, tough, and durable quality, and much valued for a variety of purposes. From its non-liability to split by any sudden shock, it is much used for lining stone-carts and barrows, for boat-building, and even in the construction of small ships; also in mill-work, turnery, and coopery;

and its lightness recommends it for the handles of hay-rakes and other rustic implements. The wood of the White Willow has been extensively used in the manufacture of chip-hats, for which purpose young branches are taken and cut into thin slices by an instrument called a shave; and these are further divided into narrow filaments by a steel comb with sharp teeth, which is passed longitudinally down the slice. The smaller rods and twigs, either with or without their bark, are made into baskets for domestic use; or, when split into two or more pieces, are applied to more ornamental purposes, such as fancy work-baskets, reticules, &c. From the bark of the Bedford Willow, and some other species, is extracted, by a chemical process, that valuable tonic medicine called *salicine*, which has been found equally efficacious with Peruvian bark, or its essential product, *quinine*, in the cure of intermittent fevers; thus it appears that in those wet, marshy districts, where agues and other low fevers abound, Providence has placed, in the Willow, a ready and potent remedy.[1] This compensating adjustment—the juxtaposition of the disease and its remedy—is probably far more universal in

---

[1] A strong infusion (made by shredding Willow bark into a vessel, pouring on some boiling water, and letting the whole stand together till cool) has nearly the same medicinal effect as *salicine* itself, and may be substituted when that more concentrated and convenient form of the remedy cannot be quickly obtained, as must often be the case in rural districts.

THE COMMON WHITE WILLOW. 91

nature than is generally perceived and taken advantage of.

From its astringent properties, the bark of most of the Willows may be advantageously used for tanning leather.

Few trees are the resort of a greater number of insects than those of the Willow tribe, whose foliage is the food of the caterpillars of many fine moths, of which we may mention the following, as a few of the most remarkable:—the Poplar Hawk-moth, and that richly-coloured insect, the Eyed Hawk-moth; those pretty soft grey and white moths, appropriately called Puss and Kitten Moths—the Emperor Moth, the Lappet Moth, the Scarlet Tiger Moth, &c.; and, among the butterflies, we may occasionally find the caterpillars of the Comma Butterfly, the large Tortoiseshell Butterfly, and the Camberwell Beauty. Others, instead of devouring the foliage, pierce the stems, and feed upon the wood itself, causing great injury, and often entire destruction to the tree; the chief of these internal enemies being the giant caterpillar of the Goat-moth—a disagreeable-looking great creature, about three inches long, and the thickness of one's finger, of a colour that may be compared to raw beef on the back, and yellow beneath. It exhales a peculiar and most unpleasant odour, which has been compared to that of a goat (whence the name of the insect); and so powerful is it, that we have detected the presence of the insect in a tree, and when, of course, it was invisible to the eye, by this scent alone. Though common enough (far too common, a tree-grower would say), this creature is but seldom seen, except by those engaged in felling and cutting up timber; we have, however, occasionally detected it wandering round the tree-trunk that had been its habitation, in search of a spot in which to undergo its change to the chrysalis state, and through that to the form of a large grey moth, with brownish markings.

Those red, fleshy excrescences, so often seen on the surface of various Willow-leaves, are galls, produced by a small species of saw-fly, the grub of which may be found within. (Some of these galls are represented on the White Willow-leaf figured.)

The White, or Huntingdon Willow, as it is sometimes called, frequently attains at maturity a height of between sixty and eighty feet, with a trunk from three to four feet in diameter.

THE GOAT-WILLOW, OR SAUGH.[1]

(*Sálix cáprea.*)

This species, called also the Round-leaved Sallow, may be readily distinguished by the leaves, which are larger and broader than in any other Willow, dark-green above, but clothed with a white, cottony down on the under side; and in the very early spring, long before the leaves appear, its branches are covered with the bright-yellow blossoms, gathered in the country on the Sunday before Easter, under the name of "palms," and carried about by children in commemoration of the palms borne before our Saviour on his entry into Jerusalem.

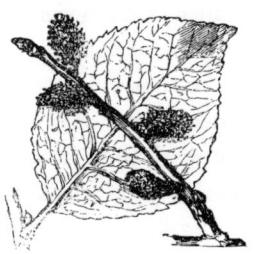

LEAF AND MALE FLOWERS OF GOAT WILLOW.

The joyous feelings inspired by the early blossoming of this Willow are thus happily expressed by Mr. Selby:—"Our associations as connected with this tree are all of a pleasing description; it reminds us, at an early period of the year, when its pure white silky catkins

---

[1] *Salix caprea.* Gen. char.: see page 86.—Spec. char.: Leaves ovate, pointed, serrated, waved-downy beneath; stipules somewhat crescent-shaped; ovary ovate, downy on a long hairy stalk; stigmas undivided, nearly sessile.

first burst the cerements that enshroud them, that the severity of winter is fast passing away, and a milder season approaching. It is also a little later, when those catkins we lately admired for their silvery lustre are now glowing with a golden inflorescence, that we first hear, and listen with pleasurable feelings beneath its richly-clothed head, to the busy hum of the honey-bee, and to that of its larger and more sonorous relative, the humble-bee, whose resuscitation from a long torpidity we have always been accustomed to hail as a certain indication of the commencement of spring, and of a mild and genial temperature." *Forest Trees.*

The Goat-willow, even when full grown, is but a moderate-sized tree, the largest specimens seldom exceeding thirty or forty feet in height; but it is more generally kept down to underwood or hedge-plant dimensions, by the constant lopping to which it is subjected for the sake of the young shoots, used for wicker-work and hurdle-making. The mature wood resembles that of the White Willow in its qualities, and is therefore applied to the same purposes, especially when its smaller size is not an objection. We may mention that the bark of this species is among the best for medicinal use in agues, &c., as a substitute for Cinchona bark.

The insects which are found on the last species are in general common to the rest of the tribe; but we must notice one interesting exception in an insect which appears to be peculiar to the Goat-Willow. This is the beautiful Lunar Hornet Sphinx (*Trochilium crabroniforme*), a moth of the clear-winged division, but which so much resembles a hornet or large wasp in its form and colouring, that it might readily be mistaken for one at first sight. If we happen to visit a Sallow plantation, at a time when the periodical fall of underwood is taking

LUNAR HORNET SPHINX; CATERPILLAR, PUPA, AND PERFECT INSECT.

place, we shall most probably find a number of the newly-cut stumps perforated with holes, just large enough to admit the tip of one's little finger, and extending downwards through the axis of the stems. These are the work of the larva of the Lunar Hornet Sphinx, a creature not at all like the generality of caterpillars, but rather resembling a large white maggot or beetle grub. This creature when young perforates the stem of the Willow near the root, and when it reaches the centre eats away a gallery, extending it upwards to the length of several inches. Having completed this toilsome process, and having arrived itself at maturity as a caterpillar, it feels the chrysalis change approaching, and at this point a curious instinct comes into play. The caterpillar has hitherto been working with its head upwards, and it will be obvious on looking at the figure, that, if the chrysalis were placed in the same position, with its head towards the closed end of the tube, the moth, on emerging, would find it a matter of great difficulty, if not an impossibility, to escape from its prison by the passage below, as the comparative rigidity of its body and wings would prevent its turning in the narrow space, so as to make its exit head foremost ; but the soft contractible caterpillar can easily manage this feat, and so providently turns head-downwards before assuming the chrysalis state, on awaking from which, the newly-formed moth makes its way into daylight, without let or hindrance. The handsome caterpillar of the Purple Emperor butterfly is said to feed chiefly on the leaves of this species.

THE COMMON OSIER.[1] (*Sálix viminális.*)

WE select this species as the most familiar example of that class of willows of humble growth, whose abundant production of long pliant shoots renders them especially valuable for all purposes of basket-making and other wicker-work; on which account they are largely cultivated in moist tracks of ground, principally by the side of rivers and streams that occasionally overflow. Such plantations, known as "Osier-beds," abound to a great extent along the banks of the Thames, between London and Reading, and often cover the "aits," or little islands that every now and then divide the stream. There are many other kinds of willow with nearly the same qualities as the present, which is the one most generally cultivated, on account of the superior vigour of its growth.

COMMON OSIER.

To enumerate the services rendered by the Osier would only be recounting the multiplied purposes of

[1] *Salix viminalis.* Gen. char.: see page 86.—Spec. char.: Leaves linear, inclining to lanceolate, very long, pointed, entire, somewhat wavy, silky beneath; branches straight and slender; ovary sessile; style as long as the undivided linear stigmas.

convenience and ornament for which wicker-work of various kinds is in hourly request, both in commerce and domestic life, from the rough hamper to the delicate and elegant appurtenances of the lady's work-table. It is to be remarked that among the very few refined accomplishments of the ancient Britons, ornamental basket-making had a prominent place, and their baskets (called in Latin "*bascandæ*") were exported to Rome, where they were held in great admiration, and commanded a high price.

Wherever the insect tribes abound, there, as a matter of course, the insect-feeding birds congregate to the banquet; and accordingly we find that willow plantations are the resort of a large company of feathered beings, who, by their constant busy movements and cheerful twitterings, give great life and interest to the scene. Here we may see in abundance those little ornithological acrobats, the Tit-mice (*Paridæ*) hanging head downwards from the swinging branches, and contorting their lithe and prettily coloured bodies into all sorts of odd postures, as they pry curiously into every nook and crevice in search of their insect friends. In the spring we may sometimes find, in considerable numbers, the nests of the Marsh Tit (*Parus palustris*), a gregarious species, which generally chooses a retired spot among willows for building in. And in such situations also, the Sedge Warblers (*Salicaria Phragmitis*), though seldom visible, may be heard uttering their varied song in chorus, and occasionally imitating the notes of the Linnet, Lark, and Swallow; while the Black-cap (*Curruca atricapilla*), and the Greater Pettichaps (*Curruca hortensis*) from their willowy bowers pour out nightly strains, hardly to be excelled in sweetness by those of Philomel herself.

THE WHITE POPLAR OR ABELE TREE.[1]

(*Pópulus álba.*)

"The Poplar, that with silver lines his leaf."—COWPER.

EVEN at a considerable distance we may recognise this tree by the peculiar effect of the white under-surface of the leaves, rendered visible by the slightest breath of wind, which also keeps the foliage in that constant quivering motion, characteristic of all the Poplars.

---

[1] *Populus alba.* Nat. order, *Salicaceæ;* Lin. syst.: *Diœcia Octandria.* Gen. char.: Barren flower, scales of the catkin lacerated; anthers, 8 to 30, arising from a turbinate, oblique, entire, single perianth. Fertile flower, scales of the catkin lacerated; perianth, turbinate, entire; stigmas 4; capsule, superior, 2-celled, 2-valved, many seeded, seeds comose.—Spec. char.: Leaves roundish, cordate, lobed, toothed, glabrous above, downy, very white beneath; fertile catkins ovate; stigmas 4.

These leaves are dark green above, and the striking contrast presented by the under side is caused by a thick coating of a snowy white, downy, or cottony substance. There is a variety of this species, very common in the country, and sometimes called the Grey Poplar (*Populus alba, v. canescens*), which has leaves more heart-shaped, and less deeply indented than that represented in the figure; and the white down being more sparing on the undersurface, gives it a greyer aspect than that of the common Abele.

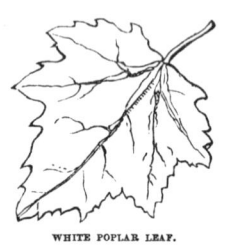

WHITE POPLAR LEAF.

The White Poplar often grows into a very large and lofty tree, the height when full grown generally varying from 80 to 100 feet. Some fine specimens, exceeding the latter altitude, may be seen on the banks of the Thames between Hampton Court and Chertsey.

From the extreme rapidity of its growth, this tree is sometimes used to form avenues and decorate pleasure-grounds in the immediate vicinity of new mansions, where it is desirable to obtain an ornamental effect in the briefest time possible, though its ultimate picturesque effect is far inferior to that of the more rich and massive trees, such as the elm and chestnut.

As a timber-tree, the White Poplar has some valuable qualities, being light, soft, and smooth, very white in colour, and with a toughness that allows nails to be driven into it near the edge without splitting, so that it is particularly adapted for packing cases. Its whiteness, and the facility with which it is scoured, render it a most excellent wood for the flooring of houses and factories, more especially as it has the property of not taking fire without great difficulty, and of burning very slowly, being in these respects the very opposite of the usual flooring material, deal, whose rapidly combustible nature is well known. This wood is also used as a substitute for that of the lime-tree by carvers and musical-instrument makers.

The foliage of the Poplars, and among them, that of the present species, is the resort of an immense number of insects, and especially of the caterpillars belonging to various moths, foremost among which is that named after this tree, the Poplar Hawk-moth, who in the caterpillar state is a fine large fellow, with a rough shagreen-like skin, of bright green colour, speckled with yellow, having seven stripes of the same placed obliquely on each side, and carrying above the tail a hard yellow horn. Occasionally these creatures abound to such an extent, as to strip the trees of their foliage, and in windy weather, as we walk beneath, a sudden gust will often whip one of them off his perch, and bring him down with a heavy thump at our feet, or on the crown of our hat, as it may happen. About midsummer, we may find on Poplar-trunks, the large moth into which this caterpillar is transformed; a pretty, but not gaily coloured insect, of greyish-brown tint, marked with red on the hind wings.

Other moths attached to the Poplar, are the Eyed Hawk-moth, with a caterpillar very much resembling the last mentioned; the Goat-moth, the Iron Prominent and Pebble Prominent moths, with their grotesque, humpbacked caterpillars, outvied, however, in personal singularity, by those of the Puss-moth,[1] which are not at all uncommon on the Poplar; the Copper Underwing, Herald-moth, Poplar Lutestring-moth, &c. The caterpillar of the splendid Camberwell Beauty, formerly called the Poplar Butterfly, also feeds on this tree.

On the decaying stem, or beheaded stump of the Poplar, we frequently find gigantic specimens of the Hard-tinder fungus (*Boletus igniarius*), and other large and curious agarics.

[1] Described and figured in "Common Objects of the Country."

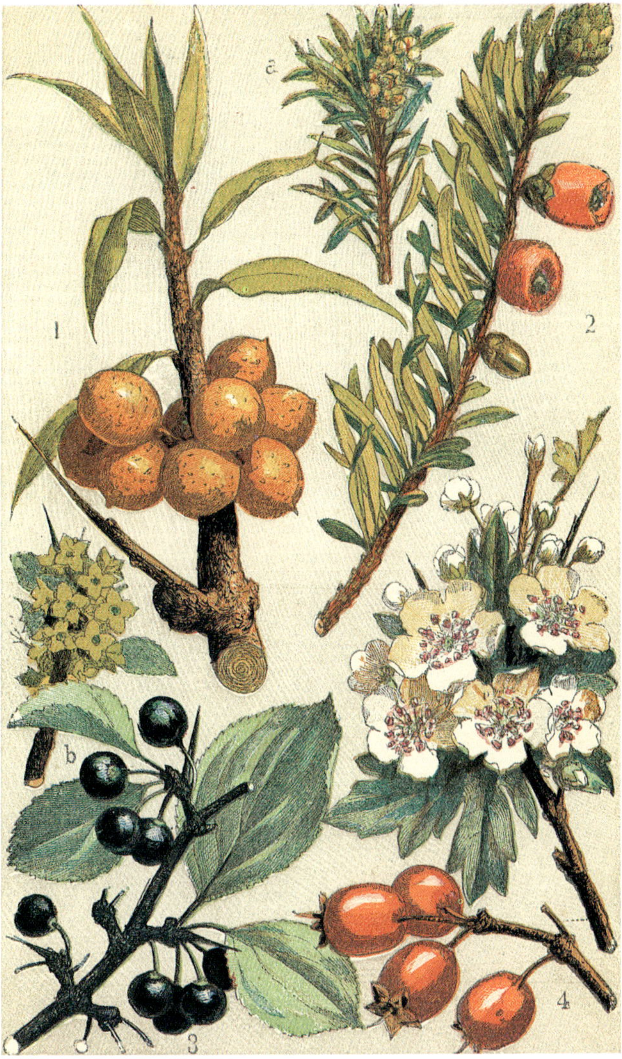
a
1
2
b
3
4

THE ASPEN, OR TREMBLING POPLAR.[1]

(*Pŏpulus trĕmula.*)

THE Aspen is a tall, straight growing tree, with considerable elegance of form; the branches stretching out horizontally, but in old trees taking a drooping character at their extremities. The leaves are rather large, and of a dark glossy green on the upper surface, and beneath of a paler tint, but not white or downy as in the last mentioned species. The peculiar tremulous motion of the foliage, which is common to all the poplars, but especially noticeable in the Aspen, is caused by the great length and slenderness of the leaf-stalks, which are also flattened vertically, giving the broad leaf such freedom of motion, that the least breath of wind sets it quivering, so that "trembling like an Aspen leaf," has passed into a proverbial com-

LEAF OF ASPEN.

---

[1] *Populus tremula.* Gen. char.: see page 99.—Spec. char.: Leaves, nearly orbicular, broadly toothed, glabrous on both sides; petioles compressed; stigmas 4-auricled at base.

parison; and numerous allusions to it are to be found among the poets, such, for instance, as that of Spenser:

> "His hand did quake
> And tremble like a leaf of Aspen green."

And the rare *stillness* of the Aspen's leaves is made by Thomson finely indicative of the breathless hush preceding a shower :—

> " Gradual sinks the breeze
> Into a perfect calm; that not a breath
> Is heard to quiver through the closing woods,
> Or rustling turn the many-twinkling leaves
> Of Aspen tall."

The qualities and uses of the timber of this tree are in most respects the same as those described under the head of the white poplar, except that it is of a much more combustible nature than the wood of that tree, or the rest of the English poplars. The insects also are generally those of the last species, but there is a kind of gnat which seems to select the leaves of the Aspen for its attacks; puncturing, and depositing its eggs, in the substance of the leaves and leaf-stalks; an operation which leads to the production of those red warty excrescences we often see on those parts.

The usual height of a full-grown Aspen is from sixty to eighty feet; but many much taller specimens are met with: one at Castle Howard, in Yorkshire, being 130 feet high, with a trunk three feet and a half thick.

THE BLACK POPLAR.[1]—(*Pópulus nígra.*)

EARLY in spring, when the branches of the Black Poplar are yet leafless, they are loaded with such a profusion of deep red catkins, or pendulous flower-spikes, that the tree, especially when lit up by the sun, presents an exceedingly rich and striking appearance, the more remarkable from the general absence of any lively tint in nature at this period. When these catkins are seen strewed on the ground beneath, as is often the case after a high wind, they have a very great resemblance to large red caterpillars in various writhing attitudes; and, if one of these is picked up and examined, it will be found to have a highly beautiful structure, and it will be then evident that the rich colouring is entirely owing to the fine red of the anthers—comparatively inconspicuous parts in the majority of flowers.

LEAF OF BLACK POPLAR.

[1] *Populus nigra.* Gen. char.: see page 99.—Spec. char.: Leaves deltoid, acute, serrated, glabrous on both sides; fertile catkins cylindrical, lax; stigmas 4.

The leaves are of a pale-green colour, with yellowish footstalks, and do not come out till the middle of May, —long after the White and Lombardy Poplars are in full foliage.

The wood of the Black Poplar is of a yellowish-white colour, and much used by turners for all kinds of white wooden vessels, such as bowls, platters, butchers' trays, &c., and for those purposes generally to which the white poplar is applicable. The young shoots may be substituted for those of the willow in basket-making. The bark of old trees, being very thick and light, is sometimes employed by fishermen, instead of cork, for supporting their line of nets in the water.

Observant readers may have noticed, on the leafstalks of this Poplar, certain large reddish-coloured protuberances of various shapes; some being almost round and berry-like, others being longer, and of twisted forms. On the under side of these will often be found an aperture, leading to a central cavity; which, on being laid open, discovers the little authors of the deformity (if such it need be called), namely, a colony of minute insects of the Aphis kind (*Aphis populi*), which are invested with such wondrous power, that, at their touch, the vegetable tissues, abandoning their own proper shapes, mould themselves into such forms as best suit the convenience and safety of these tiny magicians.

THE LOMBARDY POPLAR.[1]—(*Pópulus fastigiáta.*)

THE tall, straight, spire-like form of the Lombardy Poplar, entirely distinct from that of any other deciduous tree in the country, is so universally known, that any description of its appearance is needless for the purpose of identifying it; and the leaf so nearly resembles that of the black poplar that we deemed it unnecessary to figure it.

Familiar as this tree has now become, as a rural object and suburban ornament, we can hardly imagine that it was an exotic almost unknown in this country about a century ago, at which time plants or cuttings of it were imported from Turin.

Few trees have such a marked influence over the character of landscape scenery, especially towards the mid-distance, as the Lombardy Poplar; the towering perpendicular lines of which afford, in many situations, an agreeable relief to the prevailing flat or rounded forms with which it may be intermixed, producing the kind of effect in wooded scenes that spires and turrets do in the aspect of a city, when seen from a commanding point of view.

The graceful action of this tree, under the influence

[1] *Populus fastigiata.* Gen. char.: see page 99.—Spec. char.: Leaves smooth on each side, acuminate, serrate, deltoid, broader than long.

of the wind, is one of its peculiar charms, and has attracted the notice and admiration of poets and painters. Other trees have their *branches* waved by the zephyr, or lashed violently by the gale, but none bend with that plume-like sweep of its *whole form* that characterizes the motion of this:—

> "The Poplar's shoot,
> Which like a feather, waves from head to foot."
> *Leigh Hunt.*

The growth of this, as well as of all the Poplars, is extremely rapid; but its existence, like that of most quick-growing trees, is proportionately brief. As an instance of the celerity with which it sometimes arrives at a magnificent height, there is, or lately was, in the village of Great Tew, in Oxfordshire, a Lombardy Poplar, planted by a man who lived in a cottage within its shadow and survived to see his nursling attain the towering stature of 125 feet in the space of fifty years.

THE YEW.[1]—(*Táxus baccáta.*) (Plate F, Fig. 2.)

WHEN comparatively young, the Yew forms a pyramidal-shaped tree, maintaining this outline till it arrives at a

[1] *Taxus baccata.* Nat. order, *Taxaceæ.* Lin. syst.: *Diœcia Monadelphia.* Gen. char.: Barren flower, perianth single at

very advanced age, when it becomes a flat or round-headed tree, of low stature compared with the stoutness of its trunk, which is usually a gnarled and knotty structure, covered with reddish bark, that flakes off readily on being touched. The leaves and berries need not be here described, as they are figured in Plate F, fig. 2.

From its churchyard associations, the Yew has been generally regarded as a melancholy, funereal tree, and is addressed by one of our poets as a

> " Cheerless, unsocial plant, that loves to dwell
> 'Midst skulls and coffins, epitaphs and tombs."

But we hold other and far more pleasant feelings regarding the Yew, associating it with fair scenes in nature, where its presence had an effect the reverse of melancholy. On the picturesque banks of the Wye, for example, between Chepstow and Tintern, it abounds, and forms at all seasons a striking ornament to the limestone cliffs that overhang the river. In spring, its intensely deep green contrasts curiously with the pale-tinted verdure of the youthful vegetation around it; and in autumn, its sable depth has a still finer effect among the neighbouring rich hues of yellow, red, and

the base; stamens numerous; anthers peltate, 6 or 8-celled, cells opening beneath. Fertile flower, perianth single, urceolate, scaly; style 0; drupe fleshy, perforated at the extremity.—Spec. char.: Leaves thickly set, linear, distichous, flat; male receptacles globose.

brown, and especially when closely grouped, as we have seen it, with the bright orange clusters of the mountain ash, and with the snowy leaves and scarlet fruit of the white beam-tree. In winter, too, its evergreen quality renders it a valuable relief to the prevailing grey tones of the landscape.

The origin of the wide-spread custom of planting Yews in churchyards is involved in much uncertainty, but it is supposed that the trees often existed, before the erection of the churches, as appurtenances to the heathen places of worship, on the site of which, as it is well known, the early Christian churches were built.

Another interesting association of the Yew is with the ancient practice of archery; the Yew-bow being formerly esteemed superior to that made from any other wood; and the pages of British history, relating to times prior to the invention of gunpowder, are replete with instances of its efficiency in warfare, when wielded by the strong and dexterous hand of the English archer, to whose good service the momentous victories of Cressy, Poictiers, and Agincourt, were mainly attributed. It must be recorded also, among the chronicles of the Yew-bow, that it proved fatal to three British kings: to Harold, at the battle of Hastings; to William Rufus, in the New Forest; and to Richard Cœur de Lion, at Limoges, in France. Subsequently to the introduction of fire-arms, which nullified the military value, and

THE YEW. 111

consequent culture of the Yew-tree, it became so scarce as to be seldom procurable of sufficient length and quality for bows, and the pretty toys used in the very mild archery practice of the present day, are made of the various tough and ornamental woods imported from America.

At a comparatively recent period the Yew was a favourite garden-tree, not, indeed, for its natural and picturesque form, but as a material for clipping into the fantastic shapes of verdant sculpture that so delighted our ancestors, such as figures of nondescript birds and animals, or the more pleasing and allowable architectural forms of arcades, pyramids, cones, and the like.

In various parts of the country, but for the most part in old churchyards, are existing Yew-trees of vast antiquity, and with trunks of prodigious dimensions. Among the grandest of these ancient Yews is that in Buckland churchyard, about a mile from Dover, the trunk of which measures twenty-four feet in circumference, and is remarkable for its grotesque contortions, and the strange shapes of vegetable anatomy its parts display.

The Yew in Tisbury churchyard, Dorsetshire, is an enormous specimen, with a trunk thirty-seven feet in circumference, and having a hollow interior, entered by a rustic gate, and capable of holding several persons. Near Staines is a Yew whose age is supposed to exceed a thousand years. But, perhaps, the most remarkable

Yew in Britain is that in the churchyard of Fortingal, in Perthshire, which is supposed, on good grounds, to have been a tree at the commencement of the Christian era. It has now become a mere shell, great part of the trunk having fallen in, before which its circumference measured more than fifty-six feet.

The heart-wood of the Yew is very hard and fine-grained, qualities which, in conjunction with its exceedingly beautiful shades and veinings of rich brown and red, render it the finest of all native woods for purposes of cabinet-making and turnery-work; and the knotted root stumps of the old trees are especially curious and varied in their markings. Furniture made of Yew has also the recommendation of being entirely exempt from the attacks of insects.

The poisonous properties of Yew foliage when eaten by cattle and horses are well known; but it appears that, by mixing the leaves in gradually increasing proportions with the ordinary fodder of animals, they can at last be brought to eat it alone without any apparent ill-consequences. The deleterious effects of Yew-leaves extend to the human race also, and many melancholy instances are on record in which fatal results have followed their administration, especially to children,—for it seems that the leaves have had a considerable repute as a vermifuge. The viscid scarlet berries, however, do not share in the poisonous qualities of the foliage, and are eaten with impunity by children, who generally have a great relish for them.

No insect, so far as we are aware, feeds on any part of the Yew excepting its berries, of which wasps have been observed to be particularly fond, and their sweetness probably attracts many other species of fruit-feeding flies.

THE MISTLETOE.[1] (*Viscum álbum.*)

(Plate A, Fig. 3.)

THE Mistletoe—botanically remarkable as being the only true parasitic plant indigenous to this country, and whose associations are divided between grim traditions of Druidism and genial Christmas gaieties (to which latter its overhanging presence not a little contributes) —is in its social position familiar enough to all; but not every one has marked its curious appearance when seen

[1] *Viscum album.* Nat. order, *Loranthaceæ;* Lin. syst.: *Diœcia Tetrandria.* Gen. char.: Barren flower, calyx 0; petals 4, dilated at the base, connate, resembling a calyx; anthers sessile, adnate with the petals. Fertile flower, calyx submarginate; petals 4, dilated at the base; style 1, drupe inferior, 1-seeded.— Spec. char.: Leaves lanceolate, obtuse; stem dichotomous; heads of flowers axillary.

in the woods growing as a pendent bush from the mossy branch of an old crab-tree, its favourite situation. Here its effect is of course most striking in the winter season, when, the tree being stripped of its own leaves, those of the parasite shrub display their golden green tint most conspicuously. At this period also the pretty whitish berries are ripened, and add much to the beauty of the plant.

But the crab is not the only tree to which the Mistletoe attaches itself, as it is sometimes found wild on the thorn, poplar, willow, ash, maple, lime, and others ; occasionally also on the oak, but so rarely, that its occurrence on that tree is always looked on as a remarkable event in the annals of botany.

In Scotland the Mistletoe is almost unknown, and we believe it is there entirely confined to one locality.

From the viscid glutinous berries of the Mistletoe the adhesive substance called bird-lime has been sometimes prepared, though it is most frequently procured from the bark of the holly.

Birds of the Thrush family are especially fond of feeding on these berries, and one in particular has thence acquired the name of the Mistle-thrush (*Turdus viscivorus*).

The Mistletoe may be artificially propagated by slitting the bark of a tree, and inserting one of the seeds in the aperture, binding it over with something

THE IVY. 115

to protect the seed from the busy searching eye of birds, who would otherwise speedily transfer it to their own crops

---

THE IVY.[1] (*Hédera Hélix.*)

THIS climbing shrub, though often termed a parasitic plant, is not truly such, since it depends merely for *mechanical* support on the tree to which it attaches itself, deriving its *nourishment* honestly through the medium of its own roots in the ground; and never, as the mistletoe does, from the life-sap of the friendly tree. Still, it is probable that its closely embracing, rope-like stems, by compressing the trunk and branches, may check

LEAVES AND BERRIES OF IVY.

the flow of sap, and prevent the due expansion of the

---

[1] *Hedera Helix.* Nat. order, *Caprifoliaceæ;* Lin. syst.: *Pentandria Monogynia.* Gen. char.: Petals 5, oblong; berry 5-seeded, surrounded by the calyx.—Spec. char.: Leaves ovate, 3-5-angular and 3-5-lobed; floral, ovate, acuminate, veiny; umbels erect.

tree, causing it eventually to perish. But whatever injury it may ultimately work to the tree-owner, it is certain that its appearance, when clothing a decayed stump, or feathering the lofty stems of vigorous trees, is eminently picturesque, and that most especially in winter time, when its glossy verdure is conspicuous amid the general bareness of vegetation. Every one is familiar with, and can appreciate, the value of Ivy as an ornament to the crumbling ruins of castle or abbey, and to antique architecture of every style. Ivy, when attached to a building, has been accused of rendering it damp and hastening its decay, but the contrary of this is the truth, for it really acts as an efficient protection against the weather, adding both to the dryness and warmth of the house.

The shape of the Ivy-leaf varies very considerably (as shown in the figure above), not only on separate plants, but on different parts of the same plant; those belonging to the flowering shoots having none of that five-fingered like character of the lower leaves, but having a simply curved, ovate, or heart-shaped outline.

The pale greenish yellow flowers appear very late in the year, their season being from September to the beginning of December; and by their fragrance, and the ample store of honey in their nectaries, they attract a multitude of insects of all orders, more especially as other flowers are then scarce, so that an ivied wall in

THE IVY.

full flower forms a prolific hunting-ground for the entomologist. We have seen that lively and exquisitely tinted little insect known as the Azure-blue Butterfly (*Polyommatus argiolus*) sporting in great profusion about the ivied walls of an old Welsh castle, and as this was in July, before the appearance of the flowers, we suppose the caterpillar of this species feeds on Ivy-leaves as well as on those of the holly.

The dark-coloured berries of the Ivy, which succeed the flowers in thick and numerous clusters, remain on the plant throughout the winter, and are not fully ripe till the following spring, forming meanwhile the favourite food of many of the feathered tribe. Conspicuous among these is the Black-cap, who, after clearing away the elder-berries in the autumn, departs to winter in warmer regions, and on his return to this country in April finds a store of ripened Ivy-berries prepared, which carry him on comfortably till his insect food becomes plentiful; and it has been observed that wherever Ivy-berries abound, there will the dulcet, varied song of the Blackcap first be heard.

THE ARBUTUS, OR STRAWBERRY-TREE.[1]

(*Árbutus unédo.*)

THE beautiful Arbutus, or Strawberry-tree, can hardly be classed among native British trees, since it is never met with in a wild state in England, though in one district of the sister-isle it seems to be completely naturalized, being found in luxuriant abundance on the limestone rocks of the shore and islets of the Killarney lake, in the charming scenery of which it forms one of the choicest features. Fig. 5 on plate G represents one of the fine strawberry-like berries, the tempting appearance of which, however, is not borne out by their flavour, which is mawkish and vapid.

---

[1] *Arbutus unedo.* Nat. order, *Ericaceæ;* Lin. syst.: *Decandria Monogynia.* Gen. char.: Calyx 5-parted; corolla ovate, with a 5-cleft orifice; pellucid at base; berry 5-celled.—Spec. char.: Stem arborescent; leaves oblong, lanceolate; panicles smooth, nodding; berries many-seeded.

THE HEATH-LANDS.

IF, in the umbrageous forest, its grandeur and luxuriance of life afford us a deep, still joy, which accords well with our more pensive moods, there is, in the breezy upland Heath, an exhilarating influence, to which every lover of pure, wild nature is responsive. To our mind there is no season of the year when the high Heathland country has not its charms. Even in winter, when both flower and leaf are gone, the artist-eye rejoices in the varied effects of light and shade chasing each other over the expanse to which even the wintry tempest lends peculiar beauties : as when the overhanging storm-cloud throws the mid-distance into deep purple gloom, out of which perhaps stands, conspicuous by contrast, some lone crag gilded by a stray sunbeam ; while a foreground stretches before the artist's glance, which even at that drear season affords a rich treasury of colour, with all its endless harmonies of russet, olive, grey, and gold given by the withered heather, brakes, and other plants, still "beautiful in death," with the mosses, stones, and all the thousand accessories of a moorland scene.

Our English landscape-painters have many of them depicted in their works the finest phases of such scenery, and that with a success that testifies to their having felt to the full its magic spell. Few, if any, of the works of foreign schools come near to the best of our own in this respect. We remember none, and believe that the intense admiration and loving appreciation of beauties discoverable in the so-called "barren waste," are almost peculiarly British.

But if in winter the Heath-lands are grand and *picturable* (if we may apply that term to scenes that no picture is *able* really to represent), how much more so are they when the advancing summer clothes them with a richer beauty, bringing out in fair succession the tender verdure and lovely blossoms, and, after those- the stores of wilding fruits that especially enrich the rough mountain sides!

With spring come the delicate waxen blooms of the Bilberry, and its relatives the Cowberry, Bleaberry, Cranberry, and Bearberry. Then, a little further in the season, the near landscape is all purple and gold with the masses of Heather, Furze, and Broom. The bright air is perfumed with the breath of these, and a-hum with the song of the bee and other busy insects, who come to sip the lavish sweets of this sea of blossoms. Every sense is thus delighted, and, in such a scene and time as this the very sense of being is a joy, to those at least (and many they are, we know) whose hearts the world has not closed to all the "skyey influences" which are upon the open hill-side in summer.

In speaking of the Heath-lands, it should be observed,

that we mean generally those districts where the Heath and its companions are to be seen in perfection ; as, on the hill, or mountain-side, sometimes dry and rocky, sometimes marked with tracts of bog-land, and each situation having choice floral treasures of its own. Hither comes the botanist to seek some coveted rarity, perhaps rare to him only in his lowland home ; or the enthusiastic "fern-collector," who has journeyed some two or three hundred miles to gather with his own hands a true "British specimen" of *Amesium Germanicum*, a *Cystopteris*, or a *Woodsia*, it may be, that he hears Mr. A. has found on the sides of Ben-So-and-So ; and he must go and find it too. Well, health and success to him! and this is the place for both.

A large number of our most interesting plants, denizens of the moorlands, must here go unmentioned, since this is humbly set forth as a treatise on "Trees and Shrubs," and many of our chief favourites do not come under either of those designations. Those which do, as the Heaths, the Gorse, the Bilberry tribe, the Cloudberry, and others of the Bramble tribe, &c., we shall presently notice in detail.

In describing the Heath-land shrubs, the HEATHER itself naturally claims precedence, from its wide-spread abundance, giving name to the tracts of land it covers ;

for the beauty of its blossoms, and the manifold uses to which the whole plant is applied.

We may observe in the first place that there are three kinds of native Heaths common in Britain. One with dark green leaves, arranged in *threes* around the stem, and bearing vase-shaped blossoms of deep rich purple colour, this is called the FINE-LEAVED HEATH (*Érica cinerea.*[1])

Then there is that lovely species, the CROSS-LEAVED HEATH (*Érica tétralix*), found in moist boggy spots, and known by its delicate blush-tinted flowers, of somewhat similar shape to the last, but more globular, and arranged in a clustered head at the summit of the stem, and by its hairy leaves, grouped in *fours* round the stems.

The third and most important species, called the COMMON HEATHER or LING (*Érica vulgáris*[3]), is a plant of larger growth than the two last, and differs from them in the shape of its flowers, which are not pitcher-shaped, but have *divided* petals, forming open, bell-shaped blos-

---

[1] *Erica cinerea.* Nat. order, *Ericacæ*; Lin. syst.: *Octandria Monogynia.* Gen. char.: Sepals 4, persistent; corolla 4-cleft, persistent; filaments inserted in the receptacle; anthers bifid; capsule membranous, 4-8-celled.—Spec. char.: Anthers crested; corolla ovate; leaves 3; stigma capitate.

[2] *Erica tetralix.* Gen. char.: As above.—Spec. char.: Anthers crested; corolla ovate; style included; leaves 4-ciliated; flower capitate.

[3] *Erica vulgaris.* Gen. char.: As above.—Spec. char.: Anthers bearded, leaves opposite, sagittate.

soms of pale purplish-pink colour. All these kinds are subject to occasional variations in the colour of their flowers, which are sometimes met with, either of a pure white, or of some tint intermediate between that and their regular colour; but these varieties still preserve the usual distinctive shapes of the species to which they belong.

The Common Ling it is that constitutes the great mass of the Heather, beautiful both as a landscape feature, and in the close detail of its blossoms, and eminently useful to the inhabitants of the northern districts, where it especially abounds. In the bleak highlands of Scotland, its young shoots are almost the sole food of sheep and cattle in the winter months. Layers of Heath, intermixed with earth, are employed in forming the walls, and thatching the roofs, of the rough cabin of the highlander, and a thick bed of dry Heath often constitutes his only couch.

From the Heath blossom bees extract a great deal of honey, which is of dark colour, and possesses a very peculiar flavour, but is preferred by some palates to that furnished by the miscellaneous flowers of lowland districts.

Grouse and many other birds find secure shelter under the close branches of the Heath, and derive their chief winter support from its seeds.

The caterpillar of that fine large insect, the Oak

Egger-moth, is said to feed on the leaves of the Heath.

Besides the three commoner kinds of Heath, there are two other species, which, though belonging properly to the south of Europe, have been found wild in Cornwall, but appear to be confined to that part of the country. These are called the CORNISH MOOR HEATH (*Erica vágan*), and the CILIATE-LEAVED HEATH (*Érica ciliáris*).

THE FURZE, OR GORSE.[1]

(*Ulex Europœus.*)   (Plate G, Fig. 3.)

How admirable a plant is the Furze of our commons, with its deep, evergreen, tufted branches, radiant with golden flowers at almost every season throughout the year; and when the various heaths come into flower around it, what glorious harmonies of gold and purple do their mingled blossoms produce! Nothing but the extreme commonness of the Furze in a natural, wild

[1] *Ulex Europœus.* Nat. order, *Leguminosæ;* Lin. syst.: *Diadelphia Decandria.* Gen. char.: Calyx of 2 leaves, with a small scale at the base on each side; legume turgid, scarcely longer than the calyx.—Spec. char.: Teeth of calyx conniving; bractes ovate, loose.

THE FURZE, OR GORSE.

state, prevents its being cultivated in England among the choicest ornaments of the garden; and, in fact, it is highly valued as such in Sweden and other northern countries, where it will not grow in the open air, requiring the protection of a greenhouse to preserve it. It is said that when the famous botanist Dillenius first visited England, and saw our commons covered with the brilliant bloom of the Furze, which he had been accustomed to look on as a choice exotic, he went on his knees in grateful delight.

There is a smaller variety of the Furze, seldom exceeding two feet in height (while the ordinary kind attains to about six feet), and flowering almost exclusively in the months of September, October, and November, whereas the common Furze flowers most profusely in the early spring and summer months. By some botanists this smaller form is made a distinct species, under the name of the Dwarf Furze (*Ulex nánus*[1]).

The useful purposes to which the Furze may be applied are various. The young and tender branches form an excellent fodder for horses and cattle; bearing upon which subject, we quote the following note from a correspondent to the "Penny Magazine." "In the neighbourhood of Birmingham there are several large

[1] *Ulex nanus.* Gen. char.: See above.—Spec. char.: Teeth of calyx distant; bractes minute, oppressed.

dairy establishments in which gorse is used as an article of food. There is a small steam-engine attached to each, by which the gorse is crushed to a pulp, and in that state it is given to cows, which soon become very fond of it. A friend of mine feeds his plough-horses almost entirely on this food, and they both look and work remarkably well."

On the mountain streamlets of the Isle of Man may be seen, here and there, small water-wheels that work a pair of wooden mallets, the action of which effectually bruises the Furze-tops intended for fodder.

Furze-bushes are also planted in many places for hedges, and a Furze plantation makes a fine cover for game. In some places this plant is known by the name of Whin.

THE BILBERRY.[1]—(*Vaccinium Myrtillus.*)

(Plate D, Fig. 1.)

THE traveller in our upland and mountain districts can hardly fail to have noticed, as his almost constant com-

[1] *Vaccinium Myrtillus.* Nat. order, *Ericaceæ ;* Lin. syst. : *Octandria Monogynia.* Gen. char.: Corolla urceolate, or campanulate, 4-5-cleft, with reflexed segments; filaments inserted on the ovary; berry 4-5-celled, many seeded.—Spec. char.: Peduncles 1-flowered; leaves serrate, ovate, deciduous, stem angular.

panion, this cheerful little shrub; in spring he must have admired its rosy waxen flowers and fresh green foliage, and in autumn have eaten its refreshing fruit. It may be found in some abundance not far from London, as at Leith Hill, near Dorking, and occasionally quite in the valleys; but it flourishes best in a high airy situation, the summits of the very loftiest mountains of which this country can boast, only being too elevated for this hardy little mountaineer. It may be seen on the top of Ben Lawers, 4,000 feet above the sea.

The berries when fresh have a beautiful bloom on them; this, of course, nearly all disappears when they are brought to market, and then they are of a glossy black, like black currants. In Yorkshire, and many parts of the north, large quantities of bilberries are brought into the market, being extensively used as an ingredient in pies and puddings, or preserved in the form of jam. In Devonshire they are eaten with cream, and we can speak from personal experience of their deliciousness and wholesomeness in all these forms; and have affectionate memories, also, of many a regale on mountain-side from the *fresh* fruit with all the rich bloom upon it: much, however, of the relish of these wilding fruits must be set down to the exhilarating air and those charms of scenery that form the accessories of a mountain feast; our epicurean views might probably be greatly altered were we to taste the same fruit supplied through the medium of Covent Garden market.

One of the prettiest sights that greet our eye in the districts where it abounds, is that of a party of rustic children "a bilberrying" (for the greater portion of those that come to market are collected by children); there they may be seen, knee-deep in the "wires," or clambering over the broken grey rocks to some rich nest of berries, their tanned faces glowing with health, and their picturesque dress (or undress)—with here and there bits of bright red, blue, or white—to the painter's eye contrasting beautifully with the purple, grey, and brown of the moorland, and forming altogether rich pictorial subjects. The berries are also eaten by game, to which the dense foliage affords a secure covert; and their juice is employed to stain paper and linen of a purple colour. Goats and sheep are in some places fed on the plant, but it is rejected by horses and cows. We have seen it cultivated with a pretty effect on rock-work, &c., in a sandy peat soil.

The name varies in different districts, "Bilberry" being perhaps the most general. In some places they are called Whortleberries, in others Hurts, evidently an abbreviated corruption of the last. By the Irish they are called "Frawns."

There is another *vaccinium* that greatly resembles the Bilberry, especially in its fruits; this is—

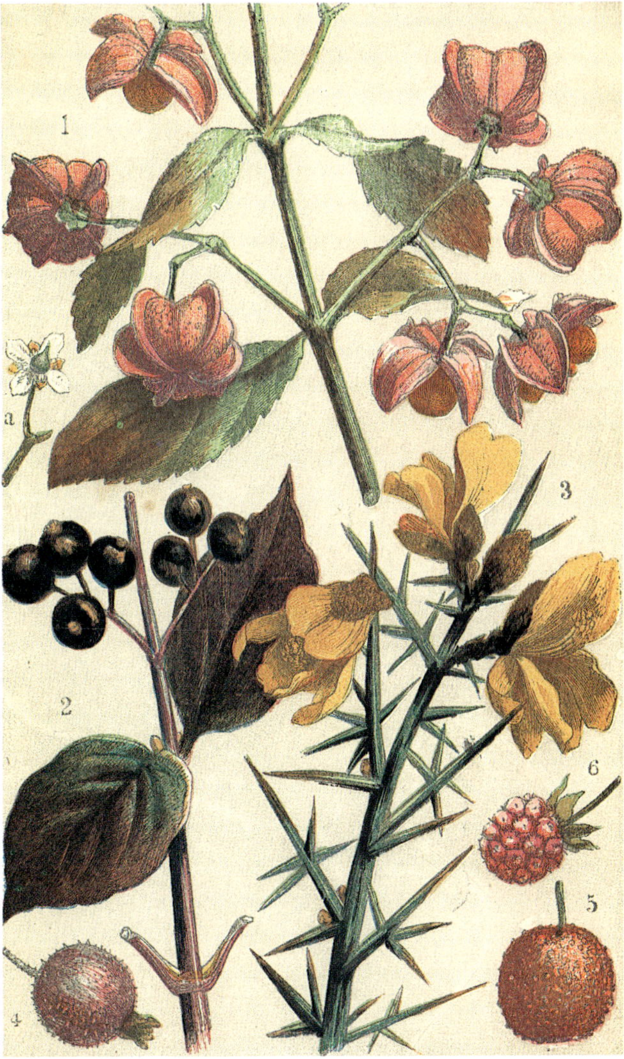
1
a
2
3
6
5
4

THE BLEABERRY, OR BOG WHORTLEBERRY [1]

(*Vaccínium uliginósum*)　(Plate D, Fig. 2),

which grows in a somewhat similar situation with the last, though its greater fondness for moisture leads it to inhabit marshy spots and mountain bogs, where it is found up to an elevation of 3,500 feet on the Scottish mountains. The flowers, which appear in April and May, come in clusters at the end of the branches, and are of a pale pink colour; and the fruit, which ripens in the autumn, is (as we before stated) like that of the Bilberry, but larger, and is black, with a glaucous bloom upon it; in taste it is tolerably agreeable, though rather insipid, and if eaten in large quantities is reputed to occasion giddiness and headache, especially if at all over-ripe.

In France, vintners use the juice for colouring their wines red, and for that purpose the berries must be innocent enough. They also furnish by distillation an ardent spirit, highly volatile and intoxicating.

This species may be readily distinguished from the Bilberry by the plain edges and downy under-surface of

---

[1] *Vaccinium uliginosum*. Gen. char.: See page 126.—Spec. char.: Leaves small, obovate, obtuse, entire, above smooth, beneath veiny, pubescent, glaucous; flower solitary; corolla urceolate.

its leaves, while those of the Bilberry have the edges toothed, and are smooth on both sides. The Bleaberry may be cultivated in gardens with the last species.

THE COWBERRY, OR MOUNT IDA WHORTLE-BERRY.[1]—(*Vaccinium Vitis Idæa.*)

(Plate D, Fig. 5.)

THIS is to our mind the most elegant of the Whortleberry group, especially when in flower. From the trailing roots rises a short stem, and from the arched extremity of this depends a cluster of elegant waxen flowers, white shaded with a delicate blush tint, and having a beautiful effect in contrast with the dark evergreen leaves. The fruit is also very pretty in its tints, particularly in its half-ripe state, the sides being then shaded, like a peach, with reddish hues of more or less intensity, in proportion as they are exposed to the sun, or shaded by overhanging leaves. When quite ripe they are of a scarlet or coral red colour, and have an acid harsh taste, with a con-

---

[1] *Vaccinium Vitis Idæa.* Gen. char.: see page 126.—Spec. char.: Dwarf; leaves obovate, emarginate, serrulate, shining above, dotted beneath; corolla cylindrical, campanulate.

siderable amount of bitterness, which renders them much less palatable than the cranberry, for which they are sometimes used as a substitute. The flowers appear in May and June, and the berries ripen from August to October. We cannot recommend the berries to be eaten uncooked, but they are sometimes made into pies in Derbyshire, and a jelly that is prepared from them is considered much preferable to that of red currant, as an accompaniment to venison. In Sweden this preserve is used medicinally for colds, sore throats, &c., for which purpose its astringency may render it really beneficial. It appears to be of much greater commercial importance in continental countries than our own. It is abundant in Scotland, Wales, and Derbyshire, and we have frequently met with it on the moors in the south of Yorkshire, growing ordinarily five or six inches from the ground, but in sandy peat it attains double that height.

We have seen a little specimen from the top of Loch-na-gar, reaching little more than half an inch from the ground, and yet bearing a full tuft of flowers.

THE CRANBERRY [1]—(*Oxycóccus palústris*)

(Plate D, Fig. 6),

Is another moorland species of the same family, producing edible berries, which have acquired a more extended reputation than those of either of its congeners, even than the bilberry; though in this country it now grows less abundantly than formerly, especially since drainage and cultivation have almost exterminated its native bogs and fens.

These valued berries are the produce of a little trailing, shrubby plant, which grows in considerable quantities in boggy places, principally in the north of England and Scotland, but also in some more southern districts, such as Norfolk, Lincolnshire, Cambridgeshire, also in Woolmer Forest, Herts. The whole plant seldom rises more than three or four inches. In May or June its delicate rose-coloured flowers are produced, somewhat resembling in shape those of the potato, the *corolla* being turned back. The fruit is ripe in August or September. As an instance of the quantity of English

[1] *Oxycoccus palustris.* Nat. order, *Ericeæ;* Lin. syst.: *Octandria Monogynia.* Gen. char.: Calyx 4-cleft; corolla 4-parted, with linear revolute segments; filaments conniving; anthers tubular, 2-parted; berry many seeded.—Spec. char.: Leaves oval, revolute at edge, acute, white beneath, segment of corolla oval.

Cranberries once furnished to the markets, it is recorded by Lightfoot, that, in the single town of Longtown, Cumberland, 20*l.* or 30*l.* worth were sold every market day throughout the season ; and during the last century those from Lincolnshire and Norfolk were sold by cartloads in Norwich. But though the demand for them still continues, the general enclosing and draining of boglands have rendered it necessary to draw on foreign markets for a supply of this fruit, which is now furnished to us by Russia, Sweden, and America, from which sources we import annually from 30,000 to 35,000 gallons. (Those from America are the fruit of another species, *O. Macrocarpus.*) The taste of the berries—doubtless familiar to many of our readers—is acid, with some astringency, and a peculiarity of flavour that causes them to be much admired by some persons, and equally disliked by others. They will keep long in bottles, if gathered dry, and closely corked. On the Continent, besides the culinary uses to which we limit the fruit, it is said to be employed by Russian bankers to whiten silver money, which they accomplish by boiling the coin in Cranberry-juice, the acid of which dissolves the superficial particles of copper alloy, leaving the surface of the silver in a state of complete purity. This pretty little plant can be easily cultivated in the garden by placing it in a dry sandy peat.

The above constitute the whole of the native members

of the Whortleberry tribe. But there is one other moorland berry-bearing plant very similar in appearance to the Cowberry, which is—

THE COMMON BEARBERRY.

(*Arctostáphylos Uva-Ursi.*)   (Plate H, Fig. 2.)

BY some botanists classed as a species of *arbutus* (already described); but as this diminutive shrub is very distinct from that tree in appearance, and seems to range naturally with the *vacciniums*, to which it is nearly related, we prefer to introduce it here under its old name.

We not uncommonly meet with this pretty plant in heathy, mountainous districts, both in Scotland, the north of England, and Wales. Its fair, pink blossoms, come out in May or June, hanging in a cluster from the end of the stem. The leaves are dark green above, lighter below. The flowers are succeeded by a group of berries, ripe in September, and then of a bright red colour, but they cannot be recommended as human food, being filled with a mealy pulp, of an austere, disagreeable taste, though they are not absolutely hurtful if eaten. They are among the berries that go to form the support of grouse, and other moorland birds, and we read that in Russia, Sweden, and America, they sometimes consti-

THE COMMON BEARBERRY.

tute the chief food of bears, whence the name Bearberry, of which both the generic and specific names are merely Greek and Latin translations; but it seems to us that so bulky a beast as Bruin, must have been put on short allowance indeed, before he could condescend to the scanty pickings held out by this tiny shrub. But though of no immediate service to us as a fruit, this plant has enjoyed a wide, and according to many accounts, a not unmerited medicinal reputation, being among the few native remedies that have not ceded to the more costly, if not more efficacious drugs from foreign countries. Its principal use is in affections of the kidneys, &c., in which cases its efficacy has been admitted by numerous members of the faculty. The leaves, which are the parts used in medicine, have a green-tea odour when dried; the plant is also used in tanning and dyeing leather. When cultivated, it makes a pretty addition to the rockery, and will thrive tolerably well in the neighbourhood of London.

THE BLACK CROWBERRY.[1]

Empétrum nígrum. (Plate D, fig. 4.)

INTERMIXED with the heather and whortleberries we often find large tufts of an under-shrub, very heath-like in its aspect, except that it bears shining black berries, that make a very conspicuous appearance when ripe; this is the Crowberry, or Crakeberry, as it is sometimes called. Early in the season it bears purplish flowers, clustered round the stem, and the berries that follow are about the size of peas, of a glossy brownish-black, with a circular dimple at the top. They are by no means palatable, although not poisonous; in fact, the Highland children make a practice of eating them; but a taste, we know, may be acquired for all sorts of queer flavours, nauseous as they may be to the untutored palate. Too great indulgence in these *delicacies,* however, is reputed to lead to head-aches, and other unpleasant symptoms; but we never pushed our experience to such an extent as to be able to speak per-

---

[1] *Empetrum nigrum.* Nat. order, *Empetraceæ;* Lin. syst.: *Diœcia Triandria.* Gen. char.: Barren flower, calyx tripartite, corolla of 3 petals; stamen 3, upon long filaments. Fertile flower, calyx tripartite, corolla of 3 petals; style very short; stigma with 6-9 rays; berry superior, globose, with 6-9 seeds. —Spec. char.: Procumbent; leaves linear, oblong.

sonally of their qualities in this respect, being contented in this, and many like cases, with the outward aspect of the plant, which is certainly very ornamental both in flower and fruit. The berries are said to be valuable medicinally, as anti-scorbutics. Moor-fowl feed on them, and they afford, when boiled with alum, a purple dye. The clan M'Lean in Scotland wear the Crowberry as their badge.

THE COMMON JUNIPER.[1]

(*Juniperus commúnis.*) (Plate D, Fig. 3.)

IN its wild state, and that in which it is usually met with, the Juniper is a low shrub, seldom more than three feet high; but when planted in a very favourable soil, it will often rise to the dimensions of a tree. At Wardour Castle, in Wiltshire, is one (the largest in England), thirty feet in height. On chalky or limestone soils we find it growing naturally, in little com-

[1] *Juniperus communis.* Nat. order, *Coniferæ;* Lin. syst.: *Diœcia Monadelphia.* Gen. char.: Barren flower, scales of the catkin subpeltate; perianth 0; stamens 4-8, 1-celled. Fertile flower, scales of the catkin few, united at length, fleshy, and surrounding the 3-seeded berry.—Spec. char.: Leaves ternate, spreading, mucronate, longer than the berry.

pact, grey-green bushes, that bear a quantity of berries, close set on the branches, some green, some brown, and others of a dark purple-black hue, and covered with a "bloom." These latter are the ripe berries, which require two seasons to arrive at maturity, so that the flower, and the green and ripe fruits, are seen together on the same bush. These berries are the parts for which the plant is almost solely valued in this country, being employed in flavouring the direful liquid yclept "gin," for which purpose several hundred tons of them are imported annually from the Continent; but even this quantity, large as it may seem, is quite insufficient to meet the enormous consumption of the fiery liquid, and the deficiency is made up by spirits of turpentine, with which all the commoner qualities of gin are partially, if not wholly flavoured. A medicinal spirit, much used in dropsical and some other complaints, is also prepared from Juniper berries.

The wood of the Juniper, from its powerfully aromatic odour, its beautiful colour, and susceptibility of high polish, is in great request with turners and manufacturers of small fancy wares.

THE BOX.[1] (*Búxus sempervírens.*)

ON Box-hill, near Dorking, in Surrey, this pretty evergreen shrub may be seen in great abundance, and growing in an apparently wild state-intermixed with low Juniper bushes; but as the above place, so far as we are aware, is the only uncultivated locality in which it is found, it can hardly be classed among our native shrubs.

The appearance of the plant requires no description, as it is universally known, in its dwarf form at least, as an edging for garden-walks and flower-beds. In a state of nature, however, it is usually seen as a round bush, or small tree.

By far the most important application of the Box in the present day, is in the art of wood-engraving, for which Box-wood is superior to any other known mate-

---

[1] *Buxus sempervirens.* Nat. order, *Euphorbiaceæ;* Lin. syst.: *Monœcia Tetrandria.* Gen. char.: Barren flower, calyx 4-leaved, 2 opposite outer ones smaller, with one bractea at the base; stamens inserted round the rudiment of a germen. Fertile flower, calyx as before, with 3 bracteas at the base; styles 3; stigmas obtuse; capsules 3-beaked, 3-celled; cells 2-seeded.— Spec. char.: Leaves oblongo-ovate, retuse, convex, glossy; their petioles slightly downy; anthers ovato-sagittate.

rial, and it is probable that the high perfection of the art, as now practised, is in a great measure due to the use made of this substance, so admirably fulfilling in every respect the requirements of the engraver. For this purpose, however, the English Box-trees are seldom of sufficient size to be available, and our great supply comes from Turkey, where the tree abounds, attaining a height of twenty-five feet, with a stem from six to nine inches thick : six or seven hundred tons of this valuable wood are annually imported from that country.

For all the finer purposes of carving, turnery, and the manufacture of mathematical instruments, &c. this clear yellow, hard, and equal-grained wood possesses a high value.

THE SWEET GALE, OR CANDLEBERRY MYRTLE.[1] (*Myrica Gále.*)

THIS shrub is one which, from its humility and sober tints, we might perhaps pass unnoticed in our mountain ram-

[1] *Myrica Gále.* Nat. order, *Myricaceæ;* Lin. syst.: *Diœcia Tetrandria.* Gen. char. : Barren flower, scales of the catkin concave ; perianth 0. Fertile flower, scales of the catkin concave; perianth, 0; styles 2; drupe 1-celled, 1-seeded.—Spec. char. : Leaves lanceolate, broader upwards, serrated, stem shrubby.

bles, were it not for the delicious balmy fragrance that it exhales, and which is alone sufficient to mark its presence, and distinguish it from every other native shrub. When the sun shines down powerfully on a bed of Sweet Gale, the whole surrounding air, to a considerable distance, becomes strongly perfumed by it. The fragrant essence resides in small vessels dotted over the surface of the yellow-green leaves, which, on being rubbed, give out their myrtle-like odour very freely.

By boiling in water the small berries which this shrub produces, a waxy or resinous substance rises to the surface, which,

LEAVES AND CATKINS OF SWEET GALE.

if procured in sufficient quantity, may be used for making candles, that, in burning, give out an agreeable, incense-like smell. From this product of its berries, the shrub is sometimes called the Candleberry Myrtle.

The leaves, which are bitter and aromatic, are occasionally used in Highland brewing as a substitute for hops; and the berries put into beer increase its intoxicating effect, in the same way as do those of *Cocculus indicus*.

The Highland clan Campbell wear the Sweet Gale as their badge.

THE LEAST WILLOW.[1] (*Sálix herbácea.*)

This pigmy species, found only in elevated mountainous situations, is chiefly remarkable as being the smallest— not only of the Willow tribe, but of all known shrubs, the adjoining figure representing an entire plant of the actual size, yet complete in all the essentials of a shrub, that is, having a woody stem and branches, &c.

THE LEAST WILLOW.

There are several other species or varieties of Willow found in similar situations to the above but we have no space to enter into a description of these, which, differ chiefly from the lowland species of this numerous and complicated family, in their diminutive size, and a few technical points interesting only to the professed botanist.

Our attention will next be claimed by the numerous species of the Bramble tribe, some of which take such a picturesque part in rustic scenery; and all of them affording a pleasant and wholesome fruit. In general

---

[1] *Salix herbácea.* Gen. char.: see page 86. Spec. char.: Leaves orbicular, somewhat retuse, serrated, shining on each side; female catkins about 5-flowered; capsule ovate, lanceolate, smooth.

they are not confined, like the whortleberries, to the moorlands and mountains, but overrun hedges and thickets in the valleys as well, with a few exceptions, of which one is

THE CLOUD-BERRY.[1] (*Rúbus Chamæmórus.*)

(Plate E, Fig. 3.)

CALLED also the Mountain Bramble and Knotberry, which we frequently meet with on the high peaty moors in the North of England, Scotland, and Wales. It would hardly be supposed, at first sight, to be a species of Bramble, being of very lowly growth, and destitute of the thorns which we associate with the tribe; but on examination, the structure of the flower, and still more, of the fruit, indicates its relationship. This little plant seldom aspires to a height of more than eight or ten inches, with a rough but not prickly stem, bearing two or three broad leaves, not at all unlike those of the mallow; and at the top of these appears a large white flower, which is succeeded by a fine pulpy fruit, of a rich orange colour when ripe (but before this of a bright scarlet tint), and of an agreeable acid taste, which has

[1] *Rubus Chamæmorus.* Nat. order, *Rosaceæ ;* Lin. syst.: *Icosandria Polygynia.* Gen. char.: Calyx 5-cleft; petals 5; berry composed of many cohering fleshy grains; receptacle nearly dry. Spec. char.: Leaves simple, lobed; stem unarmed, 1-flowered.

been compared to that of tamarinds, with less fruity richness than the raspberry, but still always welcome for its cooling refreshment to those toiling up the unshaded mountain-side. Its appearance is always striking,—the large, tempting fruit being borne by such a comparatively pigmy plant. The Cloud-berry is highly esteemed by the natives of the countries in which it abounds.

Dr. Clarke informs us that he was cured of a bilious fever by eating great quantities of this fruit in Sweden, where it probably grows more plentifully than with us. It is there much prized in the composition of soups and sauces, and is used for making vinegar.

Among the more southern localities, it has been found on the hills north of Castleton, in Derbyshire; also near Edale.

The beautiful little ARCTIC BRAMBLE[1] (*Rubus arcticus*) is too rare to be classed among the general ornaments of our mountain Heaths, but it has been found in the Isle of Mull, and in one or two other localities.

---

[1] *Rubus arcticus.* Gen. char. : see above. Spec. char. : Leaves ternate, stem unarmed ; 1-flowered.

THE STONE BRAMBLE.[1] (*Rúbus saxátilis.*)

Is likewise a native of the northern and western mountainous districts, growing in rocky places, and sometimes in dry woods. Its slender runners creep along the ground, sending up at intervals, erect shoots a span high; these are sparingly armed with weak prickles, and bear two or three threefold leaves, the stem terminated by a cluster of flowers, not showy and large, like those of the two last species, but inconspicuous, and of a greenish white colour. The fruit, when ripe, is crimson, like that of the raspberry, and very variable in shape, sometimes consisting of only one, seldom of more than three or four large grains, or drupes, as they are termed, of irregular sizes, and of an agreeably acid flavour.

THE WILD RASPBERRY.[2] (*Rúbus idœus.*)

THIS, the origin of the well-known and valued Raspberry of our gardens, is frequently to be met with in

[1] *Rubus saxatilis.* Gen. char.: see page 143.—Spec. char.: Leaves ternate, naked; runners creeping, herbaceous; panicle few-flowered.

Rubus idœus. Gen. char.: see page 143.—Spec. char.: Leaves in fives or threes, pinnated; stem erect, with small unequal prickles.

woods and thick hedges, in most parts of the country, though more abundant in the north; it may, however, be found in the immediate neighbourhood of London, in the several directions, as for instance in the vicinity of Hampstead Heath, at Blackheath, and we have found much of it in the interesting forest-ground about half-way between London and Brighton. It grows, in a wild state, to a height of three or four feet, and may be readily recognised by the cottony whiteness of the under surface of the leaves; the flowers are greenish white and very small. The fruit is like that of the cultivated sort, but smaller; the flavour, however, by no means inferior, and by many even preferred to that of the produce of the garden;—this is likewise the case with the little wild strawberry of our woods, which has been favourably compared with the monsters of Covent Garden, though the diminutiveness of the morsel is somewhat tantalising. We need not here dwell on the delicious fragrance which distinguishes this fruit, and which is familiar to every one; nor on the various uses which render the Raspberry by far the most valuable of the genus,—that is, in the cultivated state, for the wilding is not sufficiently abundant to have much importance. We are ignorant of the properties of Raspberry roots, but there is a demand for them by French cooks; what part they play in the deep mysteries of the French kitchen, we can but conjecture; some say they are made use of in dressing game. The Wild Raspberry is the food of a caterpillar that produces one of our handsomest butterflies,—the Silver-washed Fritillary (*Argynnis Paphia*),—which may be seen in its neighbourhood, winging its vigorous flight hither and thither: it is a brilliant and beautiful insect, with its rich chequering of orange, brown, and black, and the under side of its wings marked with washed stripes of silver, whence its name.

DEWBERRY, OR GREY BRAMBLE.[1]

(*Rúbus cǽsius.*)

THIS is frequently confounded with the common Blackberry, and supposed to be a luxuriantly grown variety, caused by a peculiarly favourable situation. It is, however, quite a distinct species, the most obvious difference being in the fruit, which is covered with a rich bloom, giving it an appearance of blueness wanting in the Blackberry. The flowers are of a beautiful blush-colour. The fruit, ripe in September, is generally less than that of a full-sized Blackberry; but the grains of which it

[1] *Rubus cæsius.* Gen. char.: see page 143.—Spec. char.: Stem prostrate, round, glaucous, prickly; prickles very unequal; leaves ternate; central cordate; lateral pair sessile; all wrinkled, dark green above, pubescent or hoary below; flowers corymbous; petals white.

is composed are usually much larger, and, being covered with fine bloom, give it a rich, inviting appearance, that is not disappointing on a nearer acquaintance,—the superior flavour and juiciness rendering it very preferable to the fruit of the common Blackberry. Indeed, its cultivation might be recommended on that account, as it is probable that by this means fruit of much larger size might be obtained, bearing the same proportion to that of the wild sort as the Garden Raspberry does to the wild one. The Dewberry is distributed pretty generally over the country, and there are several localities in the neighbourhood of London that furnish it.

THE COMMON BLACKBERRY, OR BRAMBLE.[1]

(*Rúbus fruticósus.*)

ALL over England, in almost every hedge and thicket, we may find the Bramble in more or less luxuriance; and, like many others of our very common plants, it has gained the distinction, which greater rarities, by their

---

[1] *Rubus fruticosus.* Gen. char.: see page 143.—Spec. char.: Stem very strong, slightly downy; prickles very broad at the base, mostly deflexed; leaves large, broadly oboval, with short, indistinct, reflected points, smooth and shining above, usually white below; panicle much branched, spreading and leafy, slightly hairy.

very infrequency, lose, of being celebrated by poet and painter, both of whom have often dwelt with delight upon the picturesque freedom of its growth, and its mingled fruit and flowers. Who, indeed, does not know what richness is given to our rural scenery, whether of mountain-side or green lane, by the tangled red stems and light sprays of the Bramble, sparkling with its frail blush blossoms, or drooping heavily with its loaded clusters of fruit of divers colours, from green through various shades of red, to the purple black of maturity? Ebenezer Elliott, one of nature's sincerest poets, has apostrophised the Bramble in some lines of great beauty, which, out of genial sympathy with their spirit, we cannot refrain from here giving at length :—

> "Thy fruit full well the school-boy knows,
> Wild bramble of the brake!
> So, put thou forth thy small white rose;
> I love thee for his sake.
> Though woodbines flaunt and roses glow
> O'er all the fragrant bowers,
> Thou need'st not be ashamed to show
> Thy satin-threaded flowers;
> For dull the eye, the heart is dull,
> That cannot feel how fair,
> Amid all beauty beautiful,
> Thy tender blossoms are!
> How delicate thy gaudy frill!
> How rich thy branchy stem!
> How soft thy voice, when woods are still,
> And thou sing'st hymns to them;

> While silent showers are falling slow,
> And 'mid the general hush
> A sweet air lifts the little bough,
> Lone whispering through the bush!
> The primrose to the grave is gone;
> The hawthorn flower is dead;
> The violet by the moss'd grey stone
> Hath laid her weary head;
> But thou, wild bramble! back dost bring
> In all their beauteous power,
> The fresh green days of life's fair spring,
> And boyhood's blossomy hour.
> Scorn'd bramble of the brake! once more
> Thou bidst me be a boy,
> To gad with thee the woodlands o'er,
> In freedom and in joy."

But beauty is not the only attribute of the Bramble, for its useful qualities are considerable. The familiar

THE PEACH-BLOSSOM MOTH.

fruit is applicable to several culinary purposes, such as for making pies and puddings, either alone or in combination with apples and other fruits, and an agreeable preserve is also prepared from it. The long pliant shoots are much used in rustic architecture for binding down thatched roofing, and in the making of beehives.

On the leaf of the Bramble feeds the caterpillar of a lovely insect, the Peach-blossom Moth, so called from the rosy spots which ornament its upper wings, and resemble the petals of the Peach-blossom, though they might with equal justice and greater poetry be compared to the blush-tinted petals of its native Bramble strewed over its dark brown wings.

THE HEDGES.

In this division of our subject will be comprised those shrubs and smaller trees that are found chiefly to compose or to ornament our English hedge-rows, whose picturesque beauty is so familiarly associated with our memories of rural delights; though, indeed, in speaking thus, we allude to those straggling, untrimmed hedges, that are supposed to betoken thriftless husbandry; for as these living fences are by no means designed by their planters for artistic effect, but solely as walls for the protection of property, it seems that their useful and picturesque qualities are antagonistic; the conditions for a model hedge, in the farmer's eye, being impenetrability, regularity, and occupance of the least possible space; whereas these perfections are precisely those that find no favour in the artistic or botanic eye.

But what scenes of quiet, rustic beauty do some of our green lanes afford, winding mazily through their free-growing, tangled hedges, which each succeeding season bedecks with its peculiar gifts, of blossom, leaf, or berry!

Early spring brings the snow-white blossoms of the Black-thorn, followed by the Hawthorn's richer wreaths. Summer gives its wild Roses and Woodbine, making the green lane a very Eden with their perfume and their beauty. Then autumn loads the hedge-shrubs with a liberal store of berries of every hue,—rich scarlet "hips and haws;" the blue-black fruits of the Buckthorn and the Sloe; the coral-like clusters of the Guelder Rose, and its relative, the Wayfaring-tree; the rosy, waxen, flower-like capsules of the Spindle-tree, and many others, —the mingled brilliance of whose colours almost compensates the eye for the vanished blossoms of summer. A large number of these bright berries continue to enrich the hedges far into the winter, forming a bright bouquet for Christmas, and some of them remain till *in sese vertitur annus,* and Spring resumes her cheerful reign.

THE HAWTHORN, OR WHITETHORN.[1]

(Cratægus Oxyacantha.)   (Plate F, Fig. 4.)

Our hedges in May can boast no ornament at all comparable to the Hawthorn, whose blossoms, by their exquisite fragrance, their snowy beauty, and their early blooming, render it the universal favourite among our wild shrubs; while poets have long sung the praises of the sweet May-blossom, identifying it even in name with the fair month of its birth.

It is not often, however, that the Hawthorn is in flower by the *first* of May. We know that formerly, in decking the May-pole, a branch of May-blossom was considered essential to crown the flowery column; but for the last hundred years—that is, ever since the alteration of the style, which places May-day eleven days earlier in the year than before that change—the Hawthorn has not frequently been found in blossom by that day; although in Gilbert White's Calendar of Nature we find the earliest observed time of its flowering marked

[1] *Cratægus Oxyacantha.* Nat. order, *Rosaceæ;* Lin. syst.: *Icosandria Di-pentagynia.* Gen. char.: Calyx 5-toothed; petals spreading, orbicular; ovary 2-5-celled; styles smooth; apple fleshy, oblong, closed by the teeth of the calyx, or by the thickened disk; putamen bony. Spec. char.: Leaves obtuse, subtrifid, serrated, smooth; peduncule and calyx nearly smooth; sepals lanceolate, acute.

as happening on April 20th; but in another season it was as late as the 10th of June.

Occasionally, when the Hawthorn grows on a clayey soil, its flowers are found to be tinged with pink, and sometimes to have a full red, or almost scarlet colour. The "Red May" of our pleasure-gardens is derived from some of these originally wild varieties.

The Hawthorn is also as variable in its fruit as in its flowers, being now and then found bearing woolly fruit, and again, with a golden yellow fruit, which produces a remarkably rich appearance in the late autumn and winter. The usual colour of these berries, or "haws," as they are called, is a deep, bright red, and dear is their aspect to many a hard-pressed bird, who finds them his chief solace and support through the pinching winter months.

The foliage of the Hawthorn, remarkable for its elegance, is the chosen food of a great number of interesting insects, principally the caterpillars of various *lepidoptera.*

Several species of these are of a gregarious nature, living together in extensive colonies under a thick network of silk, which serves them for a common protection while feeding on the foliage enclosed with themselves in the silken tent.

Among these social net-weavers are the caterpillars of a fine insect, the Black-veined White Butterfly (*Pieris*

Cratægi), a rarity in some districts, but in certain localities, and at certain periods, abounding to such an extent as entirely to strip the Hawthorn hedges of their foliage. Similar depredations are committed by the gaily-coloured progeny of the common Lackey Moth, and of the Gold-tailed, and Brown-tailed Moths; but the most formidable devastators, though the tiniest individually, are the little Ermine Moths (*Yponomeuta*), small silvery grey creatures, minutely spotted with black. The curious twig-like caterpillars of the Brimstone Moth[1] (a pretty canary-coloured creature, with brown markings), and of several other *geometers*, are common upon the Hawthorn.

THE HOLLY.[2] (*Ilex Aquifólium.*)

(Plate A, Fig. 4.)

While the hawthorn is pre-eminent for beauty among the spring blossoms of our hedges, the Holly holds a place no less distinguished among their winter adorn-

[1] *Vide* "Common Objects of the Country." Plate C, fig. 3 and 3A, and description.

[2] *Ilex Aquifolium.* Nat. order, *Aquifoliaceæ*; Lin. syst.: *Tetrandria Tetragynia.* Gen. char.: Calyx 4-5-toothed; corolla rotate, 4-cleft; style 0; berry 4-seeded.—Spec. char.: Leaves ovate, acute, spiny, shining, waved; flowers axillary, umbelled.

ments; but its familiar beauties need not here be descanted upon, as there are few English homes which are not annually graced by the presence of its growing coral berries and glistening deep green foliage.

The white flowers of the Holly, which appear in May, are clustered round the young branches, in the same position, of course, as the berries that eventually proceed from them.

There are varieties of the Holly with yellow, and also with white berries, the former having in particular a very curious and ornamental appearance. Other varieties have the leaves marked with stripes or blotches of white or yellow; and one, called the Hedgehog Holly, is distinguished by the singular character of its leaves, which are armed with spines, not only on their edges, but over the entire upper surface, so as to present no very unapt resemblance to a hedgehog.

When growing in favourable soil, and left to assume its natural size and form, the Holly sometimes attains the dimensions of a large tree, and then, especially in winter, when covered with thousands of clustered berries, forms one of the most splendid objects in nature. The chief *use* of the Holly is for making hedges, for which purpose it is surpassed by no other plant, as it forms an impenetrable fence, always green and beautiful throughout the year.

The wood of the Holly is very hard and of fine texture;

exceedingly white, so as almost to resemble ivory; takes a fine polish, and can be readily stained of various colours; so that from the possession of so many good qualities it is a wood highly valued by artisans in various departments of industry; for instance, in cabinet-making, it is admirable for veneering, and inlaying, in contrast with darker woods; the turner forms it into various delicate articles of his craft; and a large number of the handles of metal teapots and other utensils, are made of Holly-wood, stained black, in which state it affords a very good substitute for ebony.

From the bark of the young shoots of the Holly the birdlime, used by bird-catchers and gardeners, is principally obtained, by a process of maceration and trituration; though the manufacture is not by any means so extensively pursued as formerly.

Few plants are more entirely exempt from the attacks of insects than the Holly,—yet the leaves are said to be the food of the caterpillar of the pretty Azure-blue butterfly (*Polyommatus Argiolus*).

THE HAZEL.[1] (*Córylus Avellána.*)

(Plate B, Fig. 1.)

The Hazel, though it sometimes becomes a moderate-sized tree, from twenty to thirty feet in height, is far more generally known as a hedge or coppice shrub, and as such is placed here among others of that class.

Those who like ourselves have been, in their early youth at least, familiar with the pleasures of a country life, will well remember the romantic delights of " going a-nutting," when first the rich clusters became embrowned at their tips, a token of their readiness for the gathering. Full happy days were those, and the Hazel in autumn still has power to awaken their pleasant memories within us. Late in the year, too, the foliage of the Hazel-coppice has a fine effect, as the leaves assume a rich golden yellow tint, and remain on the branches till the season has very far advanced. But not only in autumn is the Hazel an interesting rural

[1] *Corylus Avellana.* Nat. order, *Corylaceæ;* Lin. syst.: *Monœcia Polyandria.* Gen. char.: Barren flowers in a cylin: drical catkin, its scales 3-cleft; perianth 0; stamens 8; anthers 1-celled. Fertile flower, perianth obsolete; germens several, surrounded by a scaly involucre; stigmas 2; nut 1-seeded, surrounded at the base with the enlarged united coriaceous scales of the involucre.—Spec. char.: Stipules oblong-obtuse, leaves roundish-cordate pointed; involucre of fruit campanulate, rather spreading, torn at margin.

object; for in earliest spring, often before the snows of winter have cleared away, its long pendulous tassels or catkins waving in the wind, are among the first evidences of nature's awakening life. These catkins are the male flowers of the Hazel, and are far more conspicuous than the female flowers, which appear at the same time, and which, though comparatively seldom observed, on account of their minuteness, are really very beautiful objects. They are to be found seated on the sides of the twigs, in the form of little scaly buds, from the points of which proceed tufts of vivid crimson threads, which are the stigmas of the enclosed flowers. One of these is shown at Plate B, Fig. 1a.

The filberts and cob-nuts of our gardens are supposed to be merely varieties originating in the common Hazel.

The long pliant shoots which the Hazel produces in great abundance are used for making crates, hurdles, hoops, fishing-rods, and various other purposes in which flexibility, toughness, and regularity of size are desirable qualifications. Hazel rods, when cut of uniform thickness, and varnished, make admirable garden-seats, and rustic flower-baskets, the design of which may be agreeably varied by combining peeled and unpeeled rods, or those with barks of different shades, so as to produce striking geometric patterns. Hazel nuts, either as luxuries or staple provender, are held in great esteem by various small animals, from school-boys, squirrels, and the like, down to the corpulent white grub that we so often turn out of a cracked nut instead of the expected kernel. This portly individual, soft and tender as he now is, would, if left undisturbed, have eventually turned into a curious beetle, of stony hardness, greyish-brown colour, and furnished with an extraordinarily long nose or beak. In this state the insect is called the Nut Weevil, and scientifically *Balaninus nucum*.

Several species of birds, whose bills are strong enough to crack or perforate the hard protecting nut-shell, feed on its contents. One of these is the Nuthatch (*Sitta Europæa*), a prettily-tinted and interesting bird, whose energetic hammering is a frequent sound in the vicinity of Hazel plantations. Sometimes the bird selects the crevice of a rough tree-trunk, sometimes the weather-worn, gaping top of an old fence-post, in which to wedge the nut that is to be attacked. We remember watching the labours of a Nuthatch who had chosen the latter position for his workshop, and on going up to the place after his departure finding the ground below strewed plentifully with the fragments of demolished nut-shells.

The leaves of the Hazel are also the *pabulum* of a large number of insects, principally the caterpillars of various Moths, though one Butterfly, namely, the Comma, is on its "free-list."

Among the Moths are those known in the fanciful

phraseology of collectors as the Lobster Moth, the Iron-prominent Moth, the Lunar Marbled-brown Moth, the Kentish Glory Moth, the Tau Emperor Moth, the Brown-muslin Moth, the Nut-tree Tussock Moth, the Copper-underwing Moth, the large Emerald Moth, the Dark-bordered Beauty Moth, the May High-flyer Moth, the Dark Oblique-bar Moth, the Great Chequered Moth, &c.

THE BIRD CHERRY.[1] (*Prúnus Pádus.*)

(Plate B, Fig. 4.)

IN many parts of the country the hedges are commonly adorned by this very pretty shrub, or small tree, which in spring is noticeable for its copious sprays of white flowers, and in autumn for its pendant bunches of fruit, black when quite ripe, but previously passing through various tints of green and red. The foliage is bright and luxuriant, so that during the greater portion of the year the Bird-Cherry forms a pleasant and picturesque object.

[1] *Prunus Padus.* Nat. order, *Rosaceæ;* Lin. syst.: *Icosandria Monogynia.* Gen. char.: Calyx 5-cleft; petals 5; drupe with a hard smooth nut.—Spec. char.: Flowers racemose, racemes pendulous, leaves deciduous, doubly serrated, somewhat rugose; petioles with 2 glands.

The uses of the Bird-Cherry to mankind are of no great importance, but its wood is held in some esteem among turners and cabinet-makers, being hard, and richly coloured and veined.

The fruit is not fit for human eating, being nauseous in flavour, and probably dangerous in its effects if taken in large quantities; it is nevertheless used to communicate a pleasant flavour to spirits.

Ten or twelve feet is the usual height of a full-grown Bird-Cherry tree, when in a state of nature, but in cultivation it sometimes reaches more than double that height.

THE SLOE, OR BLACKTHORN.[1] (*Prúnus spinósa.*)

(Plate B, Fig. 2.)

THIS spiny bush is commonly called the Blackthorn, in contradistinction to the whitethorn, or May-blossom—not on account of any difference in the colour of the blossom, those of the Blackthorn being, in fact, rather the whiter of the two—but because the branches of the

[1] *Prunus spinosa.* Gen. char.: See page 161.—Spec. char.: Peduncles solitary; leaves elliptic, lanceolate, pubescent beneath; branches spiny.

THE SLOE, OR BLACKTHORN.

Sloe are covered with blackish bark, while those of the hawthorn have a much lighter tint.

The Blackthorn generally flowers at the commencement of April, but sometimes at the end of March, and often before the appearance of the leaves, or when those are but partially developed. Gilbert White remarks that "this tree usually blossoms while cold north-east winds blow; so that the harsh rugged weather obtaining at this season is called by the country people blackthorn winter" (*Selborne*).

In certain spots where the Blackthorn largely prevails—as in some parts of Epping Forest—its effect on the landscape, when in full blossom, is singularly striking,—large portions of ground appearing, when viewed from a moderate distance, as if partial snow-storms had passed over them, leaving broad drifts, and loading the bushes with a wintry garment.

The fruit is a little globular black plum, covered, when just ripe, with a beautiful bloom, that gives it a fine rich blue colour; but its inviting appearance is by no means borne out by its taste, which is so immoderately sour and austere, that to swallow a morsel of one is a matter of considerable difficulty, and attended with an urgent choking sensation in the throat. Our malediction, however, does not apply to the fruit after it has been mellowed by frost, when it becomes not only endurable, but absolutely pleasant in flavour.

"Winterpicks" is a provincial synonyme for this fruit, and "winterpick-wine" takes the place of port in the rustic "cellar;" and not only there—for it appears that the cheaper kinds of so-called port consumed in this country are largely adulterated with Sloe-juice, though their indigenous origin is not so openly confessed as in the case of the honest "winterpick-wine" of the cottager.

But we have not exhausted the *commercial* virtues of the Sloe-bush, for it is a well-known fact that dried Sloe-leaves are extensively used in manufacturing or compounding tea, sold as Chinese; and though the article thus adulterated has been punningly denominated "*Sloe* poison," it probably is—if less exhilarating—quite as wholesome as the genuine leaf from Canton.

Thus we see that the simple Sloe of our hedges is verily a plant of wonderful endowments, since Chinese bohea, and the wine of Portugal, are equally procurable from its beneficent branches.

The straight shoots of the Blackthorn furnish admirable walking-sticks, ornamented throughout their length with a regular series of projections that give them a very pretty effect; and we have not heard that *these* are used in *adulterating* any kind of foreign walking-stick.

The caterpillars of several moths feed on the leaves of the Sloe, among which are those known as the Small Egger Moth, the Lobster Moth, the Figure of Eight

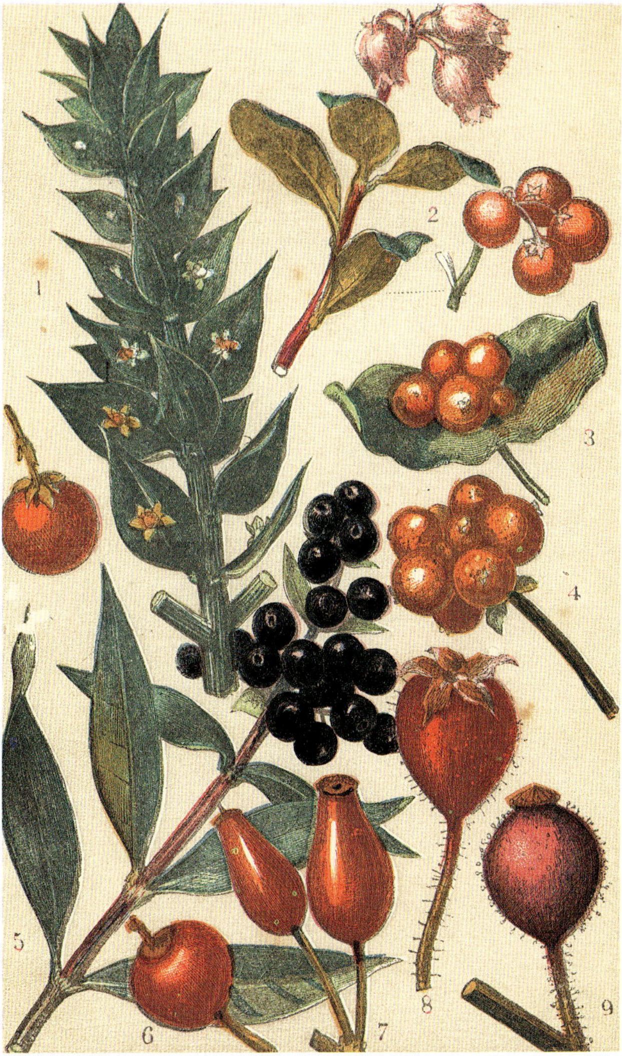

1
2
3
4
5
6
7
8
9

Moth, the Dark Dagger Moth, the Green-brindled Dot Moth, the Magpie Moth, the Brimstone Moth, &c.

THE BULLACE PLUM, sometimes recognised by botanists as a distinct species under the name of *Prunus insititia*, is probably only a variety of the common Sloe, from which it chiefly differs in the superior size of all its parts, especially the fruit, which is also frequently found of a yellow colour tinged with red, and sometimes entirely red. In taste this fruit is much less harsh than that of the Sloe, so that it may be used with advantage for culinary purposes.

THE BARBERRY.[1]   (*Bérberis vulgáris.*

(Plate B, Fig. 3.)

WE look upon the Barberry as one of the most ornamental of hedge-shrubs, either in spring, when covered with pendent branches of yellow blossoms, or in autumn, when gay with its ripened scarlet fruit. The leaves, too, are very pretty in their form, and in the cheerful

---

[1] *Berberis vulgaris.* Nat. order, *Berberaceæ;* Lin. syst.: *Hexandria Monogynia.* Gen. char.: Calyx 5-leaved; petals 6, with glands upon their claws; style 0; stigmas umbilicate; berry 1-celled, 2-4-seeded.—Spec. char.: Racemes simple, pendulous; leaves obovate, ciliate-toothed.

green tint they wear in early summer; these also possess an agreeable acid taste, and may be used in salads as a substitute for sorrel.

The berries are too powerfully acid to be eaten with pleasure in a raw state; but they are considered to be delicious when preserved or candied with sugar.

The Barberry, being furnished with close-growing, thorny branches, is well adapted to form an efficient and fruit-producing hedge; but it bears among agriculturists the reputation of producing the disease called "blight," or "rust," in the corn growing near to it; but probably the only foundation for this prejudice is the circumstance of the Barberry being itself subject to the attacks of a fungus, which covers its blossoms with a mass of orange-coloured dust, similar to that which characterises the rust in wheat; and it is evident that a Barberry-bush thus affected, and a field of rusted wheat, may exist in close proximity, without there being any relation of cause and effect between the two circumstances. We may observe, that the minute fungus just referred to as being found upon the Barberry is an extremely curious and beautiful object, when viewed by a low power of the microscope. Its scientific name is *Æcidium Berberidis*.

THE GUELDER ROSE.[1] (*Vibúrnum Opulus.*)

(Plate C, Fig. 4.)

This pretty shrub is generally to be found wild in moist hedges and in coppices by the water-side. The white flowers, which appear in May and June, are produced in flat clustered heads, the outer flowers of the cluster being much larger than the inner ones, and of a different formation, being destitute of both stamens and pistils. The beautiful Guelder Rose, or Snowball-tree, of our gardens is merely a variety of this, having *all* the flowers barren and dilated, like the outer row in the wild kind. The leaves are deeply lobed and cut, but are of variable shape. Their colour in summer is a bright green, but in autumn this changes to a beautiful crimson hue. At this season, too, its brilliant red clustered fruit forms a striking and highly ornamental feature to the hedges or thickets where the shrub occurs. Before the berries are quite ripe they are beautifully tinted with yellow on the sides least exposed to the light, and have a semi-transparent, waxen texture.

[1] *Viburnum Opulus.* Nat. order, *Caprifoliaceæ*; Lin. syst.: *Pentandria Trigynia.* Gen. char.: Corolla 5-cleft; berry with 1 seed.—Spec. char.: Leaves 3-lobed, acuminate, toothed; stalks glandular, smooth.

THE WAYFARING TREE.[1]—(*Vibúrnum Lantána.*)

THE Wayfaring Tree, belonging to the same genus as the Guelder Rose, bears a considerable resemblance to that shrub, both in its flowers and berries; but in the leaves differs entirely—those of the Wayfaring Tree being heart-shaped, finely toothed at the edges, and clothed, more especially on the under surface, with a white mealy down, which likewise extends over the branches.

WAYFARING TREE.

This shrub is plentifully met with on chalky or limestone soils. The large white flower-heads make a handsome appearance, but still more so do the berries, which at first are green, then take a fine red colour, and finally become black. In shape these berries greatly resemble those of the Guelder Rose, and in colour also—at least, in their red stage, which is the period of their greatest beauty.

---

[1] *Viburnum Lantána.* Gen. char.: see page 167.—Spec. char.: Leaves ovate, oblong, cordate, serrate, beneath rugose, with veins downy.

THE BUCKTHORN.[1] (*Rhámnus cathárticus.*)

(Plate F, Fig. 3, *b* flowers.)

In hedges and thickets throughout the country, but principally on chalky or loamy soils, we may occasionally find the Buckthorn growing in considerable plenty. It forms a shrub, or sometimes a small tree, varying in height up to a maximum of about ten or twelve feet. The branches, which are sparingly armed with short thorns, bear smooth bright green leaves, and clustered greenish yellow flowers, which are succeeded by numerous round berries of bluish black colour when ripe, and of a nauseous flavour. These berries have a violent purgative effect if swallowed, and a syrup prepared from them is sometimes used in medicine. Their juice, in combination with alum, also forms the pigment called *sap-green*, and a beautiful yellow dye is afforded by the bark.

In winter the appearance of the profuse black berries garnishing the leafless branches is conspicuously ornamental to the hedges where this shrub occurs.

[1] *Rhamnus catharticus.* Nat. order, *Rhamnaceæ;* Lin. syst.: *Pentandria Monogynia.* Gen. char.: Calyx campanulate 4-5-cleft, corolla scales protecting the stamens, inserted into the calyx; stigmas 1-2-5-cleft; berry 3-4-seeded.— Spec. char.: Spines terminal, flowers 4-cleft, diœcious; leaves ovate, stem erect, berry 4-seeded.

The foliage of the Buckthorn is reputed to be the chief food of that elegant and familiar insect, the Brimstone Butterfly, whose sportive flight on a sunny day in March, or even earlier, is among the pleasantest sights that harbinger the coming spring.

Nearly related to the common Buckthorn in its appearance, as well as in its properties, is the BERRY-BEARING ALDER, or BREAKING BUCKTHORN [1] (*Rhámnus Frángula*). It may be distinguished from the last-mentioned species by its smooth, blackish branches, destitute of thorns; its oval leaves, not toothed at the edge; its whitish flowers with purple anthers; and by the berries containing only two seeds, while those of the *common* Buckthorn contain four.

THE SEA BUCKTHORN, OR SALLOW THORN.[2]

(*Hippóphäe rhamnóides.*) (Plate F, Fig. 1.)

THOUGH abundant enough in certain localities, the sallow-thorn seems to be restricted in England to the

[1] *Rhamnus Frangula.* Gen. char.: as above.—Spec. char.: Flowers monogynous hermaphrodite; leaves entire smooth; berry 2-seeded.

[2] *Hippophäe rhamnoides.* Nat. order, *Eleagnaceæ;* Lin. syst.: *Diœcia Tetrandria.* Gen. char.: Male flowers in a catkin, tetran-

THE SEA BUCKTHORN, OR SALLOW THORN. 171

east and south-east coasts, its range extending from Yorkshire to Kent. It may be found in plenty on the sandy coast between Yarmouth and Cromer, and it grows, or was growing a few years ago, on the green sand below the church at Folkestone, also upon the sand to the east of Deal, and upon chalk at Lydden Spout.

It is a singular looking shrub, with thorny branches, remarkable silvery leaves, much whiter on the under side; and minute, inconspicuous flowers, succeeded on the female plants by fine orange-coloured fruit, or berries, that make a handsome show in the autumn, and which if not devoured by birds, remain throughout the winter. These berries have a rich juicy appearance, and are said to be pleasantly acid to the taste, and according to some accounts are not at all unwholesome, though some caution should be exercised in experimenting upon their eatable qualities, since they bear in some countries the reputation of being in a certain degree poisonous.

drous; female solitary in the axillæ of the leaves; calyx tubular, bifid at end, closed; disk 0; fruit formed of a berried calyx and akenium.—Spec. char.: Leaves linear, lanceolate, smooth above, white with scales beneath.

THE DOGWOOD, OR WILD CORNEL.[1]

(Córnus sanguínea.) (Plate G, Fig. 2.)

This common shrub of hedges and thickets is readily distinguishable by the deep red colour of its branches, and of the leaves also before the fall in autumn. The flowers, which are produced in clusters, are of a greenish white colour, and have a disagreeable odour. They are succeeded by numerous clustered, dark purplish—or almost black—berries, which are ripe in September. The taste of these is very bitter and astringent, but they abound in an oil which may be procured like that of olives by expression, and is used on the Continent for burning in lamps, and in the manufacture of soap.

The very hard wood has been applied to many minor purposes of utility, but at present its principal use seems to be in making butchers' skewers. It is said to afford the best of all charcoals for gunpowder.

In autumn and winter the appearance of the dogwood is highly ornamental to its native coppices, from the striking red hue of its branches, and the changeful

---

[1] *Cornus sanguinea.* Nat. order, *Cornaceæ;* Lin. syst.: *Tetrandria Monogynia.* Gen. char.: Involucre 4-leaved in some; calyx 4-toothed; petals 4; drupe with a 2-celled nut.—Spec. char.: Branches upright, leaves ovate, whole-coloured; cymes depressed flat.

tints of its leaves passing through various gradations, from green through purple to the intense crimson that precedes their dissolution.

THE SPINDLE-TREE.[1]

(*Euónymus europǽus.*) (Plate G, Fig. 1, *a* the flower.)

SINGULARLY beautiful as the Spindle-tree becomes in the autumn it presents nothing remarkable in its appearance earlier in the season. The small greenish white flowers appear in May, and in September the curious pendant seed-vessels ripen, remaining till midwinter on the branches, and long after the latter have become leafless. At this season few productions of nature can vie in elegance with the Spindle-tree, decorated with hundreds of these seed-vessels, or capsules, of brightest rosy pink colour and waxen texture, which, quivering on their slender footstalks, at first sight might well be taken for so many bright blossoms,—a fairy creation in that flowerless season.

[1] *Euonymus europæus.* Nat. order, *Rhamnaceæ*; Lin. syst.: *Pentandria Monogynia.* Gen.char.: Petals 5; capsule 5-cornered, 3-celled, 3-valved, coloured; seeds with an arillus.—Spec. char.: Flower stalks compressed, 3-flowered; flower usually tetrandrous; leaves oblong, lanceolate, smooth.

The resemblance to a blossom is most decided when the fully ripe capsules separate into several segments like the petals of a flower, and gaping open, expose the brilliant orange-skinned seeds within.

The declining leaves take very pretty ruddy tints, and add to the ornamental appearance of the shrub.

The wood of the Spindle-tree has been put to various uses, the chief one, and that from which it derives its name, being in the making of spindles.

The charcoal prepared from the young wood is said to be a valuable material for artists, as the marks made by it in a first sketch can, if necessary, be effaced with unusual facility.

We sometimes see the Spindle-tree in summer entirely denuded of its leaves, but clothed in their stead with a dense cobweb-like material, which is the web spun by the gregarious caterpillars of the pale-spotted Ermine Moth (*Yponomeuta euonymella*), which attacks this in common with several other hedge shrubs; and a little later in the season the little moths themselves—pretty spotted grey creatures—may be seen flitting about in myriads over the scene of their devastations.

The pretty fruit, notwithstanding its exterior loveliness, has an actively poisonous nature, producing, if swallowed, violent vomiting and other disagreeable symptoms.

Although we generally meet with the Spindle-tree in

the form of a hedge shrub, it occasionally expands into a good-sized tree, specimens having been found upwards of thirty feet in height.

A variety of the Spindle-tree is sometimes seen, having the capsules or berries pure white, and when these open, showing the strongly contrasting orange seeds, their effect is exceedingly pretty.

THE ELDER.[1] (*Sambúcus nígra.*)

This thoroughly domesticated tree, though often found apparently wild in hedges and woods, seldom wanders far from human habitations, where its presence is generally welcome—not only from its picturesque aspect, when enriched by its luxuriant cream-coloured flower-heads at midsummer, or again, by its profuse purple-black berries in autumn, but as ministering to rural comfort and conviviality in the well-known wine concocted from its berries, and on whose virtues, such as they may be, it is needless here to descant.

At no very distant period of time, the leaves, berries, flowers, and bark of the Elder, were, in some shape or

[1] *Sambucus nigra.* Nat. order, *Caprifoliaceæ;* Lin. syst.: *Pentandria Trigynia.* Gen. char.: Corolla 5-cleft; berry with 3 seeds.—Spec. char.: Cymes 5-parted; stem arborescent.

other, pressed into the service of the rustic apothecary and herbalist physician, but nearly all of its preparations have disappeared from the modern pharmacopœia.

The flowers when dried have an agreeable odour, and a fragrant water distilled from them forms a pleasantly refreshing lotion for the skin; and an infusion made by pouring boiling water on the flowers, may be taken medicinally as a powerful diaphoretic, or, in simpler language, to cause a copious perspiration.

ELDER.

The old wood of the Elder is extremely hard, and may be used generally for the same purposes as boxwood, which it much resembles in texture and colour.

The young shoots are filled with a soft pith, which, from its extreme lightness, is used in making the balls employed in electrical experiments.

Varieties of the Elder are occasionally met with, bearing fruit which when ripe is either white, or of a bright green colour, instead of the usual rich purplish-black.

WILD ROSES.

So numerous are our native Wild Roses, that we cannot attempt, in our present limited space, to particularize every species, of which there are about twenty recognised by botanists, though their distinctive characters depend for the most part on minute differences of structure, hardly appreciable by any but a botanical eye.

On Plate H we have figured four of the commoner and more distinct forms of Wild Rose fruits, which make so conspicuous an appearance in our hedges in the latter part of the year, and which bear, among country people, the general appellation of "hips."

Figure 6 (Plate H) is the globular bright-red fruit of the WHITE DOG-ROSE (*Rosa arvénsis* [1]), a very abundant species throughout the country, bearing profuse milk-white flowers, on purple foot-stalks.

Figure 7 represents the flask-shaped scarlet fruit of the COMMON DOG-ROSE (*Rosa canina* [2]), whose fair blush-blossoms so exquisitely ornament and perfume the green country lanes in summer.

---

[1] *Rosa arvensis.* Nat. order, *Rosaceæ;* Lin. syst.: *Icosandria Polygynia.* Gen. char.: Calyx urceolate, 5-cleft, fleshy, contracted at orifice; petals 5; grains bony, hairy, included in the fleshy tube of calyx.—Spec. char.: Root shoots flagelliform; prickles unequal, falcate; leaflets glaucous beneath.

[2] *Rosa canina.* Gen. char. as above.—Spec. char.: Leaflets rigid, ovate; ovaries 50-60.

Figure 8 is the somewhat egg-shaped fruit of the delicious SWEET BRIAR (*Rosa rubiginôsa*[1]),—the Eglantine of the poets,—not uncommonly found wild in various parts of the country, and so well known as a favourite inmate of our gardens. In this species the fragrance is not confined to the flowers, but extends to the leaves, which are plentifully furnished with glands containing the perfumed essence.

This glandular apparatus is still further developed in the WOOLLY-LEAVED ROSE (*Rosa tomentôsa*[2]), and several allied species or varieties, in which nearly the whole plant is covered with glandular hairs, which exhale a powerful balsamic, or resinous odour. The Woolly-leaved Rose is a beautiful species, principally found in mountainous districts; and its flowers are large and of a much deeper red than those of the common Wild Roses.

Figure 9 represents its fruit, which is covered with the gland-bearing hairs, and has a deep purplish-red colour.

The fruits of the Wild-roses in general, but principally of the Dog-rose, are used in making the preparation sold by druggists as "conserve of hips." This has a

---

[1] *Rosa rubiginosa.* Gen. char. see page 177.—Spec. char.: Prickles hooked; leaflets rugose, opaque; calyx and peduncles hispid.

[2] *Rosa tomentosa.* Gen. char. see page 177.—Spec. char.: Leaflets ovate, nearly acute; fruit hispid or naked.

WILD ROSES. 179

pleasant flavour and acid taste, but is chiefly employed as a vehicle for more powerful medicines. It is made by taking a quantity of hips when over-ripe and mellowed by frost, removing the hairy seeds from the inside, and beating up the sweet pulpy matter in a mortar with sugar.

Several interesting insects are connected with the Rose, both in a wild and cultivated state. Those beautiful productions, looking like tufts of crimson moss, and so often found on the young branches and leaf-stalks of Wild-roses, are caused by the puncture of small winged insects, similar to those that produce the galls of the oak; and if one be cut open, towards the autumn, the central part will be found to be composed of cells, each tenanted by a small white grub. These galls were formerly much used in medicine, under the name of "Bedeguar," but their reputation is now quite obsolete.

We sometimes see Rose-leaves, with circular spaces, appearing as if round pieces had been punched out of their edges. These are the work of that insect upholsterer, the Leaf-cutter Bee, who uses the pieces she cuts from the leaves as a lining for the tubular cells she excavates in the ground. The *modus operandi* of this insect is extremely curious and interesting, and we regret that we have not space to give a detailed account of it.

THE WOODBINE, OR COMMON HONEY-SUCKLE.[1] (*Lonicéra Periclýmenum.*)

THE Woodbine, whose beauty and fragrance associate it in our mind with the wild-roses—its frequent companions in our native hedge-rows—is so familiar an object that its charms require no description. Every one loves the maiden fairness and rich perfume of its blossoms, and knows the closely twining nature of the plant: how

> " With clasping tendrils it invests the branch,
> Else unadorned, with many a gay festoon
> And fragrant chaplet; recompensing well
> The strength it borrows with the grace it lends."

In the autumn and early winter the berries, represented on Plate H, fig. 4, become very ornamental. When quite ripe they are of a bright transparent cornelian red, but before that assume successively various tints of green, yellow, and orange.

In the Woodbine is seen an exemplification of that curious natural law that governs the movement of twining plants, in obedience to which the stems and

[1] *Lonicera Periclymenum.* Nat. order, *Caprifoliaceæ*; Lin. syst.: *Pentandria Monogynia.* Gen. char.: Calyx 4-5-toothed, or entire; tube of corolla long, with a 5-cleft, regular, or two-lipped limb; stamens length of corolla; stigma globose: berry distinct, 3-celled, many-seeded.—Spec. char.: Flowers capitate, terminal; leaves deciduous, all distinct.

tendrils of each species constantly twine in the same direction. The Woodbine, for instance, always twines from left to right, and the white convolvulus, or bindweed, does the same; while the black briony, an equally common plant, takes the opposite direction, twining from right to left.

The caterpillar of that elegant Butterfly called the White Admiral (*Limenitis Sibilla*), feeds upon the leaves of the Honeysuckle.

THE PERFOLIATE HONEYSUCKLE [1]

(*Lonicéra Caprifólium*)

MAY be known from the common species by the very distinct character of the leaves, the opposite pairs of which meet, and are conjoined so as to give an appearance of the stem passing through the centre of an oval leaf—technically speaking, the leaves are *perfoliate*.

This species is a doubtful native of Britain, and it is supposed that the occasional specimens found in woods and hedges are the produce of seeds brought thither from gardens by birds.

The fruit, to which the "perfoliate" leaves form a sort of dish, is represented on Plate H, fig. 3.

[1] *Lonicera Caprifolium*. Gen. char. see page 180.—Spec. char.: Flowers whorled, terminal; leaves deciduous, the upper perfoliate.

WILD CURRANTS AND GOOSEBERRIES.

(Genus *Ribes.*)

Wilding representatives of the Red and Black Currants, and of the rough and smooth Gooseberries of our gardens are frequently met with in various parts of the country, the Wild Gooseberry being by far the most common. Fig. 4, Plate G, represents the fruit of the rough Wild Gooseberry.

Several varied forms of the Red Currant have been found in mountainous woods, chiefly in the north of England, and have been looked on by some botanists as distinct species; but all of the above plants may be readily recognised, especially when in fruit, by their great resemblance to their brethren of the garden.

The botanical name of the Red Currant [1] is *Ribes rúbrum;* of the Black Currant,[2] *Ribes nígrum;* and of the Gooseberry.[3] *Ribes Grossulária.*

---

[1] *Ribes rubrum.* Nat. order, *Grossulariaceæ;* Lin. syst.: *Pentandria monogynia.* Gen char.: Petals 5, and stamens inserted into the calyx; style bifid; berry, many-seeded inferior.—Spec. char.: Berries smooth; flowers flattish; petals obcordate; leaves obtuse, 5-lobed; stem erect.

[2] *Ribes nigrum.* Gen. char. as above.—Spec. char.: Leaves dotted beneath; racemes hairy, loose; flowers campanulate; bractes shorter than flower stalks; peduncles simple at base.

[3] *Ribes Grossularia.* Gen. char. as above.—Spec. char.: Leaf stalks hairy; peduncles one-flowered; bractes 2.

THE PRIVET.[1] (*Ligústrum vulgáre.*)

(Plate H, Fig. 5.)

THIS pretty, myrtle-like under-shrub is found commonly in almost every part of the country, besides being extensively cultivated as an artificial hedge-plant, in which capacity it is excelled by few plants. It will thrive in the air of the most densely populated city; and there are abundant instances of its smoke-enduring qualities in the gardens and yards of the metropolis.

The clustered white flowers of the Privet appear about midsummer, and are very ornamental, possessing also an agreeable fragrance.

The rich masses of purple-black berries ripen in autumn, and continue to decorate the shrub during a great part of the winter, forming an attractive food for thrushes, blackbirds, finches, and other birds. An oil of good quality for burning in lamps may be obtained from these berries by bruising and submitting them to strong pressure. There are varieties of the Privet in cultivation, whose fruit when ripe is of a yellow, white, or green colour; and these, especially when contrasted

---

[1] *Ligustrum vulgáre.* Nat. order, *Oleaceæ;* Lin. syst.: *Diandra Monogynia.* Gen. char.: Corolla 4-cleft; berry 4-seeded.—Spec. char.: Leaves ellipt, lanceolate, smooth; racemes compound, dense.

with the ordinary kind, produce a very agreeable effect in the ornamental shrubbery.

To the entomologist the Privet is chiefly interesting as being the chief food of the caterpillar of that very beautiful insect the Privet Hawk Moth (*Sphinx Ligustri*).[1] The caterpillar—not at all uncommon among Privet-bushes—is a fine massive creature, exquisitely tinted with stripes of pink and white on a beautiful grass-green ground; and the moth into which he eventually is transformed,—after passing through an underground existence, as a motionless dark-brown chrysalis,—is a richly-coloured insect, the upper wings being variously shaded with brown and black, and the lower wings having a fine rose-red tint barred with black, a similar colouring extending over the body of the creature.

THE BUTCHER'S BROOM.[2] (*Rúscus aculeátus.*)

(Plate H, Fig. 1.)

BOTANICALLY speaking, the Butcher's Broom is only a half-shrubby plant, but it has so much of the aspect

[1] Both the perfect insect and caterpillar are figured in "Common Objects of the Country." Plate A, fig. 5.

[2] *Ruscus aculeátus.* Nat. order, *Asphodeleæ;* Lin. syst.: *Diœcia Monadelphia.* Gen. char.: Calyx 6-leaved; corolla 0;

THE BUTCHER'S BROOM.

and character of a shrub, and is at the same time so curious and ornamental a plant, that we are induced to include it in our list.

The most remarkable feature in the natural history of the Butcher's Broom is the peculiar situation occupied by the flower, the footstalk of which is buried under the outer coat of the leaf, so that it presents the unusual phenomenon of a flower growing out of the surface of the leaf. The flowers are small and of yellowish green colour, and the fertile ones are succeeded by large red berries, the size of small cherries, of sweet and not disagreeable taste, but of doubtful wholesomeness. The appearance of these comparatively large and richly-coloured fruits among the evergreen foliage of the plant is extremely pretty and curious.

The prickly branches were formerly used by butchers for sweeping their block, from which circumstance is derived the common English name of the plant.

male, rudiment of ovary ovate, perforated at end; female, style 1, berry 3-celled, seeds 2.—Spec. char.: Leaves mucronate, pungent, flower-bearing on the upper side and naked.

INDEX TO PLATES.

A.

1. Common, or Peduncled Oak (*Quercus pedunculata*).
2. Sessile-fruited Oak (*Quercus sessiliflora*).
3. Mistletoe (*Viscum album*).
4. Holly (*Ilex aquifolium*).

B.

1. Hazel, with Nuts (*Corylus Avellana*).
   a. Female flower of ditto.
2. Blackthorn, or Sloe (*Prunus insititia*).
   b. Fruit of ditto.
3. Barberry (*Berberis vulgaris*), flowers and fruit.
4. Bird-Cherry (*Prunus Padus*), flowers and fruit.

C.

1. White-Beam Tree (*Pyrus Aria*), flower and fruit.
2. Wild Service Tree (*Pyrus torminalis*), leaf and fruit.
3. Mountain Ash (*Pyrus Aucuparia*), leaf and fruit.
4. Guelder Rose (*Viburnum Opulus*), leaf and fruit.

D.

1. Bilberry (*Vaccinium Myrtillus*), flowers and fruit.
2. Bleaberry (*Vaccinium uliginosum*), flowers and fruit.
3. Common Juniper (*Juniperus communis*).
4. Crowberry (*Empetrum nigrum*), flowers and fruit.
5. Cowberry (*Vaccinium Vitis-Idæa*), flowers and fruit.
6. Cranberry (*Oxycoccus palustris*).

E.

1. Common Bramble, or Blackberry (*Rubus fruticosus*), flowers and fruit.
2. Dewberry (*Rubus cæsius*), fruit.
3. Cloudberry (*Rubus Chamæmorus*), flower and fruit.
4. Stone Bramble (*Rubus saxatilis*), flowers and fruit.

F.

1. Sea Buckthorn (*Hippophäe rhamnoides*), fruit.
2. Yew (*Taxus baccata*), fruit.
   a. Flowers.
3. Common Buckthorn (*Rhamnus catharticus*), fruit.
   b. Flowers.
4. Hawthorn (*Cratægus Oxyacantha*), flowers and fruit (haws).

G.

1. Spindle Tree (*Euonymus Europæus*), fruit, some expanded, showing seeds.
   a. Flower.
2. Dogwood (*Cornus sanguinea*), fruit.
3. Furze or Gorse (*Ulex Europæus*).
4. Fruit of Wild Gooseberry (*Ribes Grossularia*).
5. Fruit of Arbutus, or Strawberry-tree (*Arbutus Unedo*).
6. Fruit of Wild Raspberry (*Rubus Idæus*).

H.

1. Butcher's Broom (*Ruscus aculeatus*), flowers and fruit.
2. Bearberry (*Arctostaphylos Uva-Ursi*), flowers and fruit.
3. Fruit of Perfoliate Honeysuckle (*Lonicera Caprifolium*).
4. Fruit of Woodbine (*Lonicera Periclymenum*).
5. Fruit of Privet (*Ligustrum vulgare*).
6. Fruit of White Dog-rose (*Rosa arvensis*).
7. Fruit of Common Dog-rose (*Rosa canina*).
8. Fruit of Sweet Briar (*Rosa rubiginosa*).
9. Fruit of Woolly-leafed Rose (*Rosa tomentosa*).

APPENDIX.

The following classified list of *British lepidopterous insects,* whose caterpillars feed on the various trees and shrubs under which they are ranged, has been compiled from various authentic sources, including our own observations, and may, it is hoped, possess some interest for those readers who are attached to the pleasant pursuit of entomology; while at the same time we do not consider its introduction is foreign to the more immediate subject of this little work, since (as we have remarked in the preface) the histories of many insects are closely interwoven with those of the plants they subsist on.

The names of the plants in this list are alphabetically arranged, for more convenient reference.

ALDER.

Lime hawk moth	Smerinthus tiliæ.
Lobster m.	Stauropus fagi.
Puss m.	Cerura vinula.
Miller m.	Apatela leporina.
Iron prominent m.	Notodonta dromedarius.
Alder m.	Acronycta alni.
Dagger m.	Acronycta psi.
Scolloped hazel m.	Odontoptera bidentata.
Coxcomb prominent m.	Lophopteryx camelina.
Canary shouldered thorn m.	Geometra tiliaria.
	Geometra ulmaria.
Vapourer m.	Orgyia antiqua.
Gold-tailed m.	Porthesia chrysorrhea.
Birch mocha m.	Ephyra pendularia.
Blue bordered carpet m.	Zerena rubiginata.
Pebble hook tip	Drepana falcataria.
Silver lines m.	Hylophila quercana.

APPLE.

Wood leopard moth.	Zeuzera æsculi.
Emperor m.	Saturnia pavonia minor.
Black arches m.	Psilura monacha.
Short cloaked m.	Nola cucullatella.
Codling m.	Carpocapsa pomanella.
Brown gold m.	Acompsia unitella.
Common ermine m.	Yponomeuta padella.
Roeselian m.	Glyphipteryx roesella.
Chequered hook tip m.	Harpipteryx asperella.

ASH.

Privet hawk moth	Sphinx ligustri.
Wood leopard m.	Zeuzera æsculi.
Scarlet tiger m.	Heraclia dominula.
Red arches m.	Miltochrysta miniata.
Common footman m.	Lithosia complana.
Clifton nonpareil m.	Catocala fraxini.
Green silver lines m.	Hylophila prasinana.

BARBERRY.

Raspberry carpet moth	Anticlea berberata.
Scarce tissue m.	Triphosa cervinata.
Barberry pug m.	Eupithecia exiguata.

BEECH.

Wood leopard moth	Zeuzera æsculi.
Lobster m.	Stauropus fagi.
Iron prominent m.	Notodonta dromedarius.
Coxcomb prominent m.	Lophopteryx camelina.
Sprawler m.	Petasia cassinea.
Kentish glory m.	Endromis versicolor.
Tau emperor m.	Aglaia tau.
Black muslin m.	Penthophera nigricans.
Common quaker m.	Orthosia stabilis.
Scarce dagger m.	Acronycta auricoma.
Dagger m.	Acronycta psi.
Marvel du jour m.	Miselia aprilina.
Clifton nonpariel m.	Catocala fraxini.
Mottled umber m.	Hyhernia defoliaria.
October m.	Himera pennaria.
Great oak beauty m.	Alcis roboraria.
Dark bordered beauty m.	Epione Vespertaria.
Captain Blomer's rivulet m.	Emmelesia Blomeri.
Barred hook tip m.	Drepana unguicula.
Prominent m.	Lobophora hexapterata.
Goose feather m.	Porrectaria anatipennella.
Green silver-lines m.	Hylophila prasinaria.

BILBERRY—See WHORTLEBERRY.

BIRCH.

Camberwell beauty butterfly	Vanessa Antiopa.
Brown hair streak b.	Thecla betulæ.
Lime hawk moth	Smerinthus tiliæ.
Black and white horned clear wing m.	Ægeria sphegiformis.
Wood leopard m.	Zeuzera æsculi.
Swallow prominent m.	Leiocampa dictœa.
Coxcomb prominent m.	Lophopteryx camelina.
February prominent m.	Lophopteryx carmelita.
Lunar marbled brown m.	Drymonia chaonia.
Feathered prominent m.	Ptilophora plumigera.
Kitten moths	{ Cerura bicuspis. Cerura fuscinula. }
Kentish glory m.	Endromis versicolor.
Small egger m.	Eriogaster lanestris.
Red arches m.	Callimorpha miniata.
Black arches m.	Psilura monacha.
Large footman m.	Lithosia quadra.
Nut tree tussock m.	Demas coryli.
Red arches m.	Miltochrysta miniata.

APPENDIX. 189

Large footman moth	Œnistis quadra.
Blossom underwing m	Orthosia minosa.
Brown spot pinion m.	Orthosia litura.
Miller m.	Apatela leporina.
Scarce marvel-du-jour m.	Diphthera Orion.
Satin carpet m.	Ceratopacha fluctuosa.
Yellow horned m.	Ceratopacha flavicornis.
Dun bar m.	Cosmia trapezina.
Angle-striped sallow m.	Cosmia fulvago.
Sallow m.	Xanthia fulvago.
Light orange underwing m.	Brepha notha.
Dotted border m.	Hybernia capreolaria.
Scarce umber m.	Hybernia prosapiaria.
Mottled umber m.	Hybernia defoliaria.
Oak beauty m.	Biston prodromarius.
Peppered m.	Biston betularius.
Large emerald m.	Hipparchus papilionarius.
Dark mottled beauty m.	Alcis muraria.
Gray birch m.	Tephrosia punctularia.
Common wave m.	Cabera exanthemata.
Birch mocha m.	Ephyra pendularia.
Argent and sable m.	Melanippe hastata.
May high-flyer m.	Euthalia impluviata.
Dingy shell m.	Emmelesia heparata.
Scallop hook tip m.	Platypteryx lacertinaria.
Pebble hook tip m.	Drepana falcataria.
Oak hook tip m.	Drepana hamula.
Common fan-foot m.	Pechipogon barbalis.
Hazel tortrix m	Lozotœnia sorbiana.
Great chequered m.	Lozotœnia corylana.
Lesser long cloak m.	Antithesea pruniana.
Hoary double crescent m.	Philalcea bilunaria.
	Acrolepia betuletella.
Red barred gold m.	Eriocephala rubrifasciella.

BIRD CHERRY.

Pale spotted ermine moth	Yponomeuta euonymella.

BLACKTHORN.

Small egger moth	Eriogaster lanestris.
Lobster m.	Stauropus fagi.
Figure of 8 m.	Disphragis cœruleocephala.
Green brindled dot m.	Valeria oleagina.
Dark dagger m.	Acronycta tridens.
Streaked dagger m.	Acronycta strigosa.
Magpie m.	Abraxas grossulariata
Brimstone m.	Rumia cratægata.
Barred hook tip m.	Drepana unguicula.
Chinese character m.	Cilix compressa.
Lesser long cloak m.	Antithesia pruniana.
Clouded pearl m.	Margaritia prunalis.

BRAMBLE.

Green hair streak butterfly	Thecla rubi.
Fox moth	Lasiocampa rubi.
Black arches m.	Psilura monacha.
Chestnut m.	Glœa vaccinii.
Scarce dagger m.	Acronycta auricoma.
Bramble m.	Acronycta rumicis.

Peach blossom moth	Thyatira batis.
White spot marbled m.	Erastria fuscula.
Autumn green carpet m.	Euthalia miata.
Common oblique bar m.	Lozotœnia ribeana.
Great hook tip m.	Lozotœnia aporana.

BUCKTHORN.

Scallop brown moth	Scotosia vetulata.
Dark umber m.	Scotosia rhamnata.
Common tissue m.	Triphosa dubitata.

CHERRY.

Common quaker moth	Orthosia stabilis.

CURRANT.

Currant clear wing moth	Trochilium tipuliforme.
Large ranunculus m.	Polia flavocincta.
Clouded carpet m.	Steganolophia prunata.
Chevron m.	Electra testata
Magpie m.	Abraxas grossulariata.
Common oblique bar m.	Lozotœnia ribeana.
Gooseberry m.	Lozotœnia grossulareana.
Treble spotted black m.	Lampronia capitella.

DEWBERRY.

Scarce dagger moth	Acronycta auricoma.
Dark annulet m.	Charissa obscuraria.

ELDER.

Death's head moth	Acherontia Atropos.
Privet hawk m.	Sphinx ligustri.
Dog's tooth m.	Mamestria suasa.
Garden China mark m.	Phlyctœnia sambucalis.
Captain Blomer's rivulet m.	Emmelesia Blomeri.
Marble single dot m.	Steganoptycha unipunctana.

ELM.

Comma butterfly	Grapta comma.
Elm butterfly	Vanessa polychloros.
Lime hawk moth	Smerinthus tiliæ.
Wood leopard m.	Zeuzera æsculi.
Goat m.	Cossus ligniperda.
Buff tip m.	Hammatophora bucephala.
Gipsy m.	Porthetria dispar.
Common quaker m.	Orthosia stabilis.
Copper underwing m.	Amphipyra pyramidia.
Coxcomb prominent m.	Lophopteryx camelina.
Double-spot brocade m.	Miselia bimaculosa.
Miller m.	Apatela leporina.
White-spotted pinion m.	Cosmia diffinis.
Gold tail m.	Porthesia chrysorrhea.
Lesser spotted pinion m.	Cosmia affinis.
Brown tailed m.	Porthesia chrysorrhea.
Brick coloured m.	Orbona ferruginea.
Clifton nonpareil m.	Catocala fraxini.
Small brindled beauty m.	Nyssia hispidaria

APPENDIX. 191

Peppered moth .... Biston betularius.
Brindled beauty m. .... Biston hirtarius.
Scalloped oak m. .... Crocallis elinguaria.
Scarce magpie m. .... Abraxas ulmata.
November m. .... Oporabia dilutata.
Black-eyed marble m..................... Spilonota nigricostana.
Marbled single dot m. .... Steganoptycha unipunctana.
White treble spot m. .... Acleris cerusana.
Autumnal m. .... Argyromiges autumnella.
White-spotted black m. .... Lampronia melanella.

FURZE.

Transparent chimney-sweep moth ... Fumea radiella.
Marbled single dot m. .... Steganoptycha unipunctana.
Light-striped edge m. .... Carpocapsa ulicetana.
Robertsonian m. .... Macrochila Robertsonella.

GOOSEBERRY.

Clouded carpet moth .... Steganolophia prunata.
Chevron m. .... Electra testata.
Common oblique back m. .... Lozotœnia ribeana.
Gooseberry m. .... Lozotœnia grossulareana.

HAZEL.

Comma butterfly .... Grapta comma.
Wood leopard moth .... Zeuzera æsculi.
Lobster m...................................... Staurophus fagi.
Iron prominent m. .... Notodonta dromedarius.
Lunar marbled brown m. .... Dymonia Chaonia.
Kentish glory m............................. Endromis versicolor.
Tau emperor m.............................. Aglaia tau.
Brown muslin m. .... Psyche fusca.
Dun bar m..................................... Cosmia trapezina.
Nut tree tussock m. .... Demas coryli.
Light orange underwing m. .... Brepha notha.
Copper underwing m. .... Amphipyra pyramidia.
Large emerald m. .... Hipparchus papilionarius.
Dark bordered beauty m................ Epione vespertaria.
Common white wave m.................. Cabera pusaria.
May high-flyer m........................... Euthalia impluviata.
Broken barred carpet m................. Harpalyce corylata.
Dark oblique bar m. .... Lozotœnia heparana.
Hollow oblique bar m. .... Lozotœnia cerasana.
Great chequered m. .... Lozotœnia corylana.
Arched m. .... Roxana arcuana.
Hazel m... Semioscopis avellanella.

HEATH.

Emperor moth .... Saturnia pavonia minor.
Great egger m. .... Lasiocampa Roboris.
Transparent chimney-sweep m. ...... Fumea radiella.
True lover's knot m. .... Lycophotia porphyrea.
Beautiful underwing m. .... Anarta myrtilli.
Alternate barred m. .... Sericoris alternana.
Half brown m. .... Pœcilochroma semifuscana.
Dingy rose m................................. Cochylis subroseana.
                                      Anacampsis ericæ.

HONEYSUCKLE.

Broad bordered bee hawk moth	Sesia fuciformis.
Black chestnut m.	Glœa subnigra.
Spring carpet m.	Lobophora polycommata.
Early toothed stripe m.	Lobophora lobulata.
Forked red bar m.	Lozotœnia xylosteana.
Tooth streaked hook tip m.	Harpipteryx dentella.
Six cleft plume m.	Alucita hexadactyla.

HORNBEAM.

Scarce umber moth	Hybernia prosapiaria.
October m.	Himera pennaria.
Flounced thorn m.	Geometra carpiniaria.
Light emerald m.	Campœa margaritata.
Little emerald m.	Chlorissa putataria.
Cream short cloaked m.	Spilonota comitana.

HORSE CHESTNUT.

Wood leopard moth	Zeuzera æsculi.
Large footman m.	Œnistis quadra.
Sycamore m.	Apatela aceris.
March m.	Anisopteryx æscularia.

IVY.

Pale headed chestnut moth	Orthosia pistacina.
Lunar underwing m.	Orthosia humilis.
Tawny pinion m.	Xylina semibrunnea.
Sallow m.	Xanthia fulvago.
Flounced rustic m.	Orbona rufina.

JUNIPER.

Juniper carpet moth	Thera juniperata (and others of same genus).
Juniper pug m.	Eupithecia lævigata.
White bordered m.	Macrochila marginella.
Juniper m.	Anacampsis juniperella.

LIME.

Lime hawk moth	Smerinthus tiliæ.
Wood leopard m.	Zeuzera æsculi.
Buff tip m.	Pygœra bucephala.
Lobster m.	Stauropus fagi.
Coxcomb prominent m.	Lophopteryx camelina.
Sprawler m.	Petasia cassinea.
Kentish glory m.	Endromis versicolor.
Small egger m.	Eriogaster lanestris.
Gipsy m.	Hypogymna dispar.
Black V m.	Leucoma vau-nigrum.
Common quaker m.	Orthosia stabilis.
Pale pinion m.	Xylina petrificata.
Marvel du jour m.	Miselia aprilina.
Dagger m.	Acronycta psi.
Dun bar m.	Cosmia trapezina.
Orange m.	Xanthia citrago.
Mottled umber m.	Hybernia defoliaria.
Oak beauty m.	Biston prodromarius.
Brindled beauty m.	Biston hirtarius.

Canary shouldered thorn moth	Geometra tiliaria.
Clouded August thorn m.	Geometra angularia.
Plain August thorn m.	Geometra quercinaria.
Flounced thorn m.	Geometra carpiniaria.˙
Swallow-tail m.	Ourapteryx sambucaria.
Large emerald moth	Hipparchus papilionarius.
Scorched wing m.	Eurymene dolabraria.
November dagger m.	Diurena Novembris.
Linnæan m.	Glyphipteryx Linnæella.

MAPLE.

Maple prominent moth	Lophopteryx cucullina.
Feathered prominent m.	Ptilophora plumigera.
Sycamore m.	Apatela aceris.
Mocha m.	Ephyra omicronaria.

MOUNTAIN ASH.

Streaked dagger moth	Acronycta strigosa.
Brimstone m.	Rumia cratægata.
Light emerald m.	Campœa margaritata.

OAK.

Purple hair streak butterfly	Thecla quercûs.
Lime hawk moth	Smerinthus tiliæ.
Golden-tail clearwing m.	Trochilium cynipiforme.
Oak egger m.	Lasiocampa roboris.
Buff tip m.	Hammatophora bucephala.
Iron prominent m.	Notodonta dromedarius.
Coxcomb prominent m.	Lophopteryx camelina.
Sprawler m.	Petasia cassinia.
Great prominent m.	Petasia trepida.
Marbled brown m.	Drymonia dodonea.
Lunar marbled brown m.	Drymonia chaonia.
Kitten m.	Cerura fuscinula.
Small oak egger m.	Limacodes testudo.
Brown muslin m.	Psyche fusca.
Gipsy m.	Porthetria dispar.
Red arches m.	Miltochrysta miniata.
Common footman m.	Lithosia complana.
Large footman m.	Œnistis quadra.
Clouded drab m.	Orthosia instabilis.
Lead coloured drab m.	Orthosia gracilis.
Twice-spotted quaker m.	Orthosia munda.
Common quaker m.	Orthosia stabilis.
Blossom underwing m.	Orthosia minosa.
Copper underwing m.	Amphipyra pyramidia.
Grey shouldered knot m.	Xylina lambda.
Brindled green m.	Hadena protea.
Scarce marvel-du-jour m.	Diphthera orion.
Lesser lutestring m.	Ceratopacha diluta.
Yellow horned m.	Ceratopacha flavicornis.
Frosted green m.	Ceratopacha ridens.
Scallop winged oak m.	Cleoceris oo.
Dunbar m.	Cosmia trapezina.
Orange upperwing m.	Xantholeuca croceago
Flounced rustic m.	Orbona rufina.
Brick coloured m.	Orbona ferruginea.
Dark crimson underwing m.	Catocala sponsa.
Light crimson underwing m.	Catocala promissa.
Light orange underwing m.	Brepha notha.

Dotted border moth	Hybernia capreolaria.
Scarce umber m.	Hybernia prosapiaria.
Mottled umber m.	Hybernia defoliaria.
Pale brindled brown m.	Phigalia pilosaria.
Oak beauty m.	Biston prodomarius.
Peppered m.	Biston betularius.
October m.	Himera pennaria.
Scalloped oak m.	Crocallis elinguaria.
Flounced thorn m.	Geometra carpiniaria.
Early thorn m.	Geometra illunaria.
Purple thorn m.	Geometra illustraria.
Small emerald m.	Hemithea vernaria.
Great oak beauty m.	Alcis roboraria.
False mocha m.	Ephyra punctaria.
Scorched wing m.	Eurymene dolabraria.
November m.	Oporabia dilutata.
Common emerald m.	Chlorissa thymiaria.
Pebble hook tip m.	Drepana falcataria.
Oak hook tip m.	Drepana hamula.
Barred hook tip m.	Drepana unquicula.
Common fan foot m.	Pechipogon barbalis.
Olive crescent m.	Æthia emortualis.
Least black arches m.	Nola strigulalis.
Green silver lines m.	Hylophila prasinana.
Scarce silver lines m.	Hylophila quercana.
Hazel tortius m.	Lozotœnia sorbiana.
Dark oblique bar m.	Lozotœnia heparana.
Hollow oblique bar m.	Lozotœnia cerasana.
Forked red bar m.	Lozotœnia xylosteana.
Oak red bar m.	Lozotœnia roborana.
Ashy silver barred m.	Pseudotomia fraternana.
Green tufted m.	Leptogramma squamana.
Pale chequered m.	Oporinia tortricella.
Cramerian m.	Argyromiges Cramerella.
Thunberg's m.	Gracillaria Thunbergella.

PEAR.

Wood leopard moth	Zeuzera æsculi.
Short cloaked m.	Nola cucullatella.
Brown gold m.	Acompsia unitella.
Whitethorn bar m.	Telea cratægella.

PINE AND FIR.

Pine hawk moth	Sphinx pinastri.
Black arches m.	Psilura monacha.
Orange footman m.	Lithosia aureola.
Common footman m.	Lithosia complana.
Large footman m.	Œnistis quadra.
Barred red m.	Ellopia fasciaria.
Grey carpet m.	Thera variata (and others of the same genus). (Genus) Achatia.
Light silver striped m	Pseudotomia strobilella.
Scarce orange spotted m.	Orthotœnia geminana.
Orange spotted m.	Orthotœnia turionella.
Spotted pine m.	Orthotœnia resinella.
Streaked pine m.	Orthotœnia comitana.
Scarce ermine m.	Anesychia dodocea.
Large gray m.	Eudorea cembrella.

Resin gray moth .... Eudocea resinea.
Brown knot horn m. .... Phycita fusca.

PLUM.

Copper underwing moth .... Amphipyra pyramidia.
Dark dagger m............................... Acronycta tridens.
Early m. .... Cheimatobia rupicapraria.
Wainscot hook tip m. .... Harpipteryx scabrella.

POPLAR.

Camberwell beauty butterfly .... Vanessa Antiopa.
Poplar hawk moth .... Smerinthus Populi.
Eyed hawk m. .... Smerinthus ocellatus.
Hornet m. .... Trochilium apiforme.
Clear underwing m........................ Ægeria asiliformis.
Goat m. .... Cossus ligniperda.
Iron prominent m. .... Notodonta dromedarius.
Pebble prominent m. .... Notodonta zig zac.
Swallow prominent m. .... Leiocampa dictœa.
Coxcomb prominent m. .... Lophopteryx camelina.
Pale prominent m. .... Pterostoma palpina.
Dusky marbled brown m. .... Gluphisia crenata.
Puss m... Cerura vinula.
Kitten moths................................ { Cerura furcula.
                                                      Cerura bifida.
                                                      Cerura integra.
Ermine puss m. .... Cerura erminea.
Plain muslin m. .... Heterogenea asellus.
Common footman m. .... Lithosia complana
Dingy shears m. .... Orthosia upsilon.
Copper underwing m. .... Amphipyra pyramidia.
                                                      Clostera curtula (and others of genus).
Poplar green m............................. Acronycta megacephala.
Bramble m.................................... Acronycta rumicis.
Dagger m...................................... Acronycta Psi.
Herald m. .... Scoliopteryx libatrix.
Poplar lutestring m. .... Ceratopacha Or.
Figure of 80 m. .... Ceratopacha octogesima.
Yellow horned m........................... Ceratopacha flavicornis.
Olive m. .... Plastenis subtusa.
Clifton nonpareil m. .... Catocala fraxini.
Orange underwing m..................... Brepha Parthenias.
March dagger m........................... Diurene fagella.
Pale oak beauty m......................... Alcis consortaria.
Poplar m. .... Electra populata.
Small Phœnix m............................ Harpalyce silaceata.
Pebble hook tip m. .... Drepana falcataria.
Gold fringe m. .... Hypsopygia costalis.
Cream spotted sable m. .... Microsetia trimaculella.
Agaric m. .... Euplocamus mediellus.
                                                      (Genus) Harpagus.
Poplar slender m........................... Gracillaria præangusta.

PRIVET.

Privet hawk moth .... Sphinx ligustri.
Coronet m. .... Acronycta ligustri.
Brindled beauty m. .... Biston hirtarius.

Lilac beauty moth	Pericallia syringaria.
Brindled-barred yellow m.	Lobophora viretata.
Rosy flounced m.	Agrotera flammealis.

RASPBERRY.

Chalk carpet moth	Zerene procellata.
Rose tortrix m.	Lozotœnia nebulana
Great brown m.	Lozotœnia rosana.

WILD ROSE.

Shoulder stripe moth	Lampropteryx badiata.
Streamer m.	Anticlea derivata.
Oblique bar m.	Lozotœnia lævigana.
Rose tortrix m.	Lozotœnia nebulana.
Great hook tip m.	Lozotœnia oporana.
Great brown m.	Lozotœnia rosana.
Brown cloaked m.	Spilonota aquana.
The Bergmannian m.	Argyrotoza Bergmannana.

SPINDLE.

Death's head moth	Acherontia Atropos.
Scorched carpet m.	Zerene adustata.
Pale-spotted ermine m.	Yponomeuta euonymella.

SYCAMORE.

Buff tip moth	Pygœra bucephala.
Sycamore m.	Apatela aceris.

WALNUT.

Wood leopard moth	Zeuzera æsculi.
Peppered m.	Biston betularius.

WHITETHORN.

Small egger moth	Eriogaster lanestris.
Lappet m.	Gastropacha quercifolia.
Figure of 8 m.	Disphragis cœruleocephala.
Brown muslin m.	Psyche fusca.
Small oak egger m.	Trichiura cratægi.
Green brindled crescent m.	Miselia oxyacanthæ.
Lackey m.	Clisiocampa neustria.
Brown tail m.	Porthesia auriflua.
Gold tail m.	Porthesia chrysorrhœa.
Dark dagger m.	Acronycta tridens.
Pale brindled beauty m.	Phigalis pilosaria.
Lunar thorn m.	Geometra lunaria.
Brimstone m.	Rumia cratægata.
Barred straw m.	Electra pyraliata.
Pinion spotted pug m.	Eupithecia consignata.
Common emerald m.	Chlorissa thymiaria.
Crimson and gold m.	Pyrausta purpuralis.
Hazel barred m.	Lozotœnia cratægana.
Common ermine m.	Yponomeuta padella.
Whitethorn bar m.	Telea cratægella.
Lesser tawny crescent m.	Batis lunaris.
Varied knot horn m.	Phycita hostilis.
Feathered twin spot m.	Incurvaria pectinella.
Red-barred gold m.	Eriocephala rubrifasciella.

WHORTLEBERRY.

Chestnut moth	Glœa vaccinii.
Beautiful yellow underwing m.	Anarta myrtilli.
Little thorn m.	Epione advenaria.
Bilberry m.	Sericoris myrtillana.

WILLOW.

Camberwell beauty moth	Vanessa Antiopa.
Elm or large tortoiseshell butterfly	Vanessa polychloros.
Comma b.	Grapta comma.
Poplar hawk moth	Smerinthus populi.
Eyed hawk m.	Smerinthus ocellatus.
Goat m.	Cossus ligniperda.
Emperor m.	Saturnia pavonia minor.
Lappet m.	Gastropacha quercifolia.
Pebble prominent m.	Notodonta zig zac.
Swallow prominent m.	Leiocampa dictœa.
Coxcomb prominent m.	Lophopteryx camelina.
Pale prominent m.	Pterostoma palpina.
Small chocolate-tip m.	Clostera reclusa.
Chocolate-tip m.	Clostera curtula.
Kitten moths	Cerura bicuspis. Cerura furcula. Cerura arcuata. Cerura integra.
Puss m.	Cerura vinula.
Brown muslin m.	Psyche fusca.
Scarlet tiger m.	Heraclia dominula.
Satin m.	Leucoma salicis.
Common quaker m	Orthosia stabilis.
Brown spot pinion m.	Orthosia litura.
Powdered quaker m.	Orthosia sparsa.
Red line quaker m	Orthosia lota.
Dingy shears m.	Orthosia upsilon.
Miller m.	Apatela leporina.
Poplar green m.	Acronycta megacephala.
Herald m.	Scoliopteryx libatrix.
Double kidney m.	Plastenis retusa.
Minor shoulder-knot m.	Cleoceris viminalis.
Barred sallow m.	Xanthia aurago.
White wave m.	Cabera pusaria.
Red underwing m.	Catocala nupta.
Orange underwing m.	Brepha parthenias.
Scalloped hazel m.	Odontopera bidentata.
Early thorn m.	Geometra illunaria.
Pale oak beauty m.	Alcis consortaria.
Striped twin spot m.	Cidaria salicata.
Bordered beauty m.	Epione apiciaria.
Peacock m.	Macaria notata.
Lesser bell m.	Colobochyla salicalis.
Small green oak m.	Earis chlorana.
White backed m.	Antithesia salicella.
Dingy straw m.	Cleodora salicella.
Brindled white back ermine m.	Ederesa curvella.
Cream spotted sable m.	Glyphipteryx Linnæella. (Genus) Harpagus.

The above list refers to the Willows in general, but the insects in the following list are those found more particularly on the

GOAT WILLOW OR SALLOW.

Purple emperor butterfly	Apatura Iris.
Lunar hornet sphinx moth	Trochilium crabroniforme.
	Gastropacha ilicifolia.
Feathered prominent m.	Ptilophora plumigera.
Broad-barred kitten m.	Cerura latifascia.
Lead-coloured drab m.	Orthosia gracilis.
Twin-spotted quaker m.	Orthosia munda.
Small quaker m.	Orthosia cruda.
Early grey m.	Hadena lithorhiza.
Pink-barred sallow m.	Xanthia flavago.
Small seraphim m.	Lobophora sexalisata.
Pebble hook tip m.	Drepana falcataria.
Retuse marble m.	Philalcea subocellana.
Short gold bar m.	Argyrosetia semifasciella.